PSYCHOANALYSIS AND CONTEMPORARY THOUGHT

PSYCHOANALYSIS AND CONTEMPORARY THOUGHT

By
D. W. Winnicott, John Bowlby, Ilse Hellman,
Marion Milner, Roger Money-Kyrle,
Elliott Jaques, Joan Riviere

With an Introduction by
Sylvia Payne

Edited by
John D. Sutherland

Essay Index Reprint Series

 BOOKS FOR LIBRARIES PRESS
FREEPORT, NEW YORK

Originally published by
The Hogarth Press and The Institute of Psycho-Analysis
as No. 53 in the International Psycho-Analytical
Library, London

Reprinted 1971 by arrangement with
The Hogarth Press, Ltd.

INTERNATIONAL STANDARD BOOK NUMBER:
0-8369-2373-1

LIBRARY OF CONGRESS CATALOG CARD NUMBER:
75-134139

PRINTED IN THE UNITED STATES OF AMERICA

EDITORIAL NOTE

As part of the celebrations of the centenary of Freud's birth, members of the British Psycho-Analytical Society gave six public lectures in the Friends House, London, on 'Psycho-Analysis and Contemporary Thought', during April and May 1956. The large numbers who attended these lectures were a notable tribute to Freud, to the increasing impact of his work, and to the lecturers. Many of those who heard the lectures expressed the wish to have them in print, and this volume is to meet their wish.

The order of the lectures has been altered for publication. Dr. Winnicott's paper, the most purely psycho-analytical one, deals with the early development of one of man's most characteristic emotions, the sense of guilt, and is presented first. The two lectures broadly concerned with other aspects of child development, viz., 'Psycho-Analysis and Child Care' and 'Psycho-Analysis and the Teacher' then follow. The rest of the series, devoted to certain contemporary problems to which psycho-analysis has made, or can make, an important contribution, is given in its original order.

Dr. Payne's preliminary remarks to the lectures make an appropriate introduction and, as a postscript, there is included the brief paper which Mrs Riviere contributed at the end of the last lecture.

J. D. SUTHERLAND

CONTENTS

LIST OF ILLUSTRATIONS

INTRODUCTION

By Sylvia M. Payne, c.b.e., m.b., b.s.

The year 1956 included the centenary of Sigmund Freud's birth. To anticipate and to prepare for the celebrations to be held on May 6th, his birthday, the British Psycho-Analytical Society decided to arrange a series of lectures to give the public the opportunity of hearing of the influence which Freud's original work has had on contemporary thought and on the cultural activities of the present day. The fact that Freud's original work can contribute to the understanding of these different cultural interests, as well as to the treatment of mental illness, is an indication of the value of his discoveries.

Biologists have shown us that it was the attainment of the power of speech and the use of language and conceptual thought which form the basis of man's biological dominance, and that the hope of evolutionary progress is in the region of mental development.

The capacity to communicate in words made it possible to describe action instead of performing it, to speak of feelings and emotions instead of acting them out, to learn by recorded experiences of the past and to increase the power to predict the future.

Going hand in hand with the power to verbalise was the realisation of self (which can be called self-consciousness) and the development of self-identity. The function of symbolisation arose with these aspects of mental development—language itself is symbolism.

Freud's recognition of the language of the unconscious has given us access to the phases of mental development, which lead up to and involve the beginning of speech in the individual. He found, as the result of his researches, that in human infancy and childhood the mind has a vivid imagination stimulated by the tension of innate impulses, perceptions, and infantile experiences. These imaginings, often expressed by bodily reactions and not verbalised nor conscious, tend to be progressively repressed and forgotten as development proceeds. It seems likely that the human offspring's prolonged dependence on parents because of the years necessary to reach maturity, in contrast to the speedy maturity of animals, is closely connected with man's psychical development.

Although no longer conscious in adult life, the imaginings and memories of infantile experiences, particularly when associated with anxiety, have a profound influence on subsequent mental development, and help to determine the character of personal and social relationships, cultural interests, and the way of living.

The ability to understand what the young child is communicating, whether verbalised or acted out, is obviously of great value. In the case of the adult, in whom the infantile mental processes which have survived as such are now unconscious, the ability to interpret these increases man's ability to communicate with his fellows. He learns a new language through the discovery of a capacity to read his own unconscious. The process involves an increase in knowledge of the self and an enlargement of consciousness, and can be compared with the psychological effect of the first use of language, to which I have already referred, when self-consciousness and the recognition of identity and individuality were established in the human psyche. Julian Huxley says 'conscious and conceptual thought is the latest step in life's progress'. Freud's recognition and exploration of the unconscious has made it possible to increase the individual's capacity for conscious and conceptual thought by dealing with the unconscious causes of interference with an individual's mental development. It is not my intention to imply that Freud's recognition of the significance of unconscious mental processes has initiated a genetic change in the evolution of the mind of man, because there could be no evidence of this kind at the present time. It may, however, be regarded to be what Huxley calls a 'modificational substitute' for genetic change.

The progressive effect of Freud's work must depend on the continuation of research on unconscious processes. We are still in the phase of research which needs time and protection from the increasing tendency in the world to swamp individualism by denial of differences and the mass approach to problems in every walk of life.

Some of Freud's work has already become an accepted part of our knowledge of the mind; for example, the concept of the unconscious mind. I can remember in the 1920s that, except for a few psychiatrists, poets, and artists, people were shocked and rejected the idea of an unconscious.

I first met Professor Freud at an International Psycho-Analytical Congress in Berlin in 1922. I have still a clear visual memory of him as I listened and watched him deliver a profound and original speech without a written note, expressed in simple language in a voice which in itself was worth listening to. I should like to quote here something Freud said himself about his work:

> I became a doctor through being compelled to deviate from my original purpose, and the triumph of my life lies in my having, after a long and roundabout journey, found my way back to my earliest path. . . . In my youth I felt an over-powering need to understand something of the riddles of the world in which we live and perhaps even to contribute something to their solution. The most hopeful means of achieving this end seemed to be to enrol myself in the medical faculty.

We know that he carried out his researches on the mentally sick, and through the study of their dreams and symptoms, listening with infinite patience to whatever they could communicate to him, he began to be able to interpret the language of the unconscious; but only because he was struggling at the same time to interpret his own unconscious.

Apart from his great gifts, I think honesty and integrity were his greatest character traits. He was an example of that rare variety of the human race, namely a man with the creative gifts of the artist and the mental development of the scientist.

Some men are immortal owing to the impression made by personality, others by the power for good or evil which they wielded over other men. A few never die because they have read some secret of the universe and handed down the knowledge to posterity.

Sigmund Freud is one of this group of immortals.

I

PSYCHO-ANALYSIS AND THE SENSE
OF GUILT

By DONALD W. WINNICOTT, F.R.C.P.

IN this lecture I shall reach to no more profound statement
than that of Burke who wrote two hundred years ago that
guilt resides in the intention. The intuitive flashes of the
great, however, and even the elaborate constructs of poets
and philosophers, are lacking in clinical applicability;
psycho-analysis has already made available for sociology
and for individual therapy much that was previously locked
up in remarks like this one of Burke.

A psycho-analyst comes to the subject of guilt as one who
is in the habit of thinking in terms of growth, in terms of the
evolution of the human individual, the individual as a
person, and in relation to the environment. The study of the
sense of guilt implies for the analyst a study of individual
emotional growth. Ordinarily, guilt feeling is thought of as
something that results from religious or moral teaching.
Here I shall attempt to study guilt feeling, not as a thing to
be inculcated, but as an aspect of the development of the
human individual. Cultural influences are of course important, vitally important; but these cultural influences can
themselves be studied as an overlap of innumerable personal
patterns. In other words, the clue to social and group
psychology is the psychology of the individual. Those who
hold the view that morality needs to be inculcated teach
small children accordingly, and they forgo the pleasure of
watching morality develop naturally in their children, who
are thriving in a good setting that is provided in a personal
and individual way.

I shall not need to examine variations in constitution.
We have indeed no clear evidence that any individual who

is not mentally defective is constitutionally incapable of developing a moral sense. On the other hand, we do find all degrees of success and failure in the development of a moral sense. I shall attempt to explain these variations. Undoubtedly there are children and adults with a defective guilt sense, and such defect is not specifically linked with intellectual capacity or incapacity.

It will simplify my task if I divide my examination of the problem into three main parts:

(1) The sense of guilt in those individuals who have developed and established a capacity for guilt feeling.

(2) The sense of guilt at the point of its origin in individual emotional development.

(3) The sense of guilt as a feature conspicuous by its absence in certain individual persons.

At the end I shall refer to the loss and recovery of the capacity for guilt sense.

1. *A Capacity for Sense of Guilt Assumed*

How does the concept of guilt appear in psycho-analytic theory? I think I am right in saying that the early work of Freud in this field had to do with the vicissitudes of guilt-sense in those individuals in whom a capacity for guilt-sense could be taken for granted. I will therefore say something about Freud's view of the meaning of guilt for the unconscious in health, and the psycho-pathology of guilt-sense.

The work of Freud shows how it is that true guilt resides in the intention, in unconscious intention. Actual crime is not the cause of guilt feeling; rather is it the *result* of guilt—guilt that belongs to criminal intention. Only legal guilt refers to a crime; moral guilt refers to inner reality. Freud was able to make sense of this paradox. In his early theoretical formulations he was concerned with the id, by which he referred to the instinctual drives, and the ego, by which he referred to that part of the whole self that is related to the environment. The ego modifies the environment in order to bring about id-satisfactions, and it curbs id-impulses in order that what the environment can offer can be used to best advantage, again for id-satisfaction. Later (1923) Freud used the term super-ego to name that which is accepted by the ego for use in id-control.

Freud is here dealing with human nature in terms of *economics*, and deliberately simplifying the problem for the purpose of founding a theoretical formulation. There is an implied determinism in all this work, an assumption that human nature can be examined objectively and can have applied to it the laws that are known to apply in physics. In ego-id terms the sense of guilt is very little more than *anxiety with a special quality*, anxiety felt because of the conflict between love and hate. Guilt-sense implies tolerance of ambivalence. It is not difficult to accept the close relationship between guilt and the personal conflict that arises out of coincident loving and hating, but Freud was able to trace the conflict to its roots and to show that the feelings are those associated with the instinctual life. As is now well-known, Freud found in analysis of adults (neurotic rather than psychotic) that he regularly came back to the early childhood of the patient, to intolerable anxiety, and to the clash of love and hate. In the simplest possible terms of the Oedipus complex, a boy *in health* achieved a relationship with his mother in which instinct was involved and in which the dream contained an in-love relationship with her. This led to the dream of the death of the father, which in turn led to the fear of the father and the fear that the father would destroy the child's instinctual potential. This is referred to as the castration-complex. At the same time there was the boy's love of the father and his respect for him. The boy's conflict between that side of his nature which made him hate and want to harm his father, and the other side by which he loved him, involved the boy in a sense of guilt. Guilt implied that the boy could tolerate and hold the conflict, which is in fact an inherent conflict, one that belongs to healthy life.

This is all quite simple, except that only through Freud has it been recognised that in health the climax of anxiety and guilt has a date; that is to say, has a first vitally important setting—the small child with biologically-determined instincts living in the family and experiencing the first triangular relationship. (This statement is purposely simplified, and I shall not make any reference here to the Oedipus complex in terms of sibling-relationships, nor any statement of the equivalent to the Oedipus complex in a child brought up away from the parents or in an institution.)

In the early psycho-analytic statement there is but little reference to the destructive aims in the love impulse, or to the aggressive drives that only in health become fully fused with the erotic. All this needed eventually to be brought into the theory of the origin of guilt, and I shall examine such developments later. In the first statement guilt arises out of the clash of love and hate, a clash which is inevitable if loving is to include the instinctual element that belongs to it. The prototype has reality at the toddler age.

All psycho-analysts are familiar in their work with the replacement of symptoms by the more normal development, a sense of guilt, and an increased consciousness and acceptance of the content of the phantasy which makes the sense of guilt logical. How illogical the sense of guilt can seem! In Burton's *Anatomy of Melancholy* there is a good collection of cases illustrating the absurdities of guilt feeling. In long and deep analysis patients feel guilt about anything and everything, and even about early environmental adverse factors that we can easily discern as chance phenomena. Here is a simple illustration:

A boy of eight became increasingly anxious, and eventually ran away from school. He was found to be suffering from an unbearable sense of guilt because of the death of a sibling that took place some years *prior to his own birth*. He had recently heard about this, and the parents had no idea that he was disturbed by the news. In this case it was not necessary for the boy to have a long analysis. In a few therapeutic interviews he discovered that the crippling sense of guilt which he felt about this death was a displacement from the Oedipus complex. He was a fairly normal boy, and with this amount of help he was able to return to school, and his other symptoms cleared up.

The Super-ego

The introduction of the concept of the super-ego (1923) was a big step forward in the inevitably slow evolution of psycho-analytical metapsychology. Freud had done the pioneer work himself, bearing the brunt when the world was disturbed by his drawing attention to the instinctual life of children. Gradually other workers gained experience through the use of the technique, and Freud had many colleagues by the time he used the term super-ego. With his new term, Freud was indicating that the ego, in coping with the id, employed certain forces which were worthy of a name. The child gradually acquired controlling forces. In the over-simplification of the Oedipus complex, the boy introjected the respected and feared father, and therefore carried about with him controlling forces based on what the child perceived and felt about this father. This introjected father-figure was highly subjective, and coloured by the child's experiences with father-figures other than the actual father and by the cultural pattern of the family. (The word introjection simply meant a mental and emotional acceptance, and this term avoids the more functional implications of the word incorporation.) A sense of guilt therefore implies that the ego is coming to terms with the super-ego. Anxiety has matured into guilt.

Here in the concept of the super-ego can be seen the proposition that the genesis of guilt is a matter of inner reality, or that guilt resides in the intention. Here also lies the deepest reason for guilt feeling related to masturbation and the auto-erotic activities generally. Masturbation in itself is no crime, yet in the total phantasy of masturbation is gathered together all the conscious and unconscious intention.

From this very much simplified statement of the psychology of the boy, psycho-analysis could begin to study and examine the development of the super-ego in both boys and girls, and also the differences that undoubtedly exist in the male and female in regard to super-ego formation, in the pattern of conscience, and in the development of a capacity for guilt-feeling. Out of the concept of the super-ego a great deal has developed. The idea of the introjection of the father-figure has turned out to be too simple. There is an early history of the super-ego in each individual: the introject may become human and father-like, but in earlier stages the super-ego introjects, used for control of id-impulses and id-products, are sub-human, and indeed are primitive to any degree. Thus we find ourselves studying guilt-sense in each individual infant and child as it develops from crude fear to something akin to a relationship to a revered human being, one who can understand and forgive. (It has been pointed out that there is a parallel between the maturing of the super-ego in the individual child and the development of monotheism as depicted in early Jewish history.)

All the time while conceptualising the processes which underlie the sense of guilt we are keeping in mind the fact that the sense of guilt, even when unconscious and even when apparently irrational, implies a certain degree of emotional growth, ego health, and hope.

The Psycho-pathology of Guilt-sense

It is common to find people who are burdened by a sense of guilt and indeed hampered by it. They carry it round like the load on the back of Christian in *Pilgrim's Progress*. We know that these people have a potentiality for constructive effort. Sometimes when they find a suitable opportunity for constructive work the sense of guilt no longer hampers them and they do exceptionally well; but a failure of opportunity may lead to a return of guilt-feeling, intolerable and inexplicable. We are dealing here with abnormalities of the super-ego. In successful analysis of individuals who are oppressed by a sense of guilt, we find a gradual lessening of this burden. This lessening of the burden of guilt-feeling follows the lessening of repression, or the approach of the patient towards the Oedipus complex and an acceptance of responsibility for all the hate and love that this involves. This does not mean that the patients lose the capacity for a sense of guilt (except in so far as in some cases there may have been a false super-ego development based in an abnormal way on the intrusion of a very powerful authoritarian influence derived from the environment of early years).

We can study these excesses of guilt-feeling in individuals who pass for normal, and who indeed may be among the most valuable members of society. It is easier, however, to think in terms of illness, and the two illnesses that must be considered are melancholia and obsessional neurosis. There is an interrelationship between these two illnesses, and we find patients who alternate between one and the other.

In obsessional neurosis, the patient is always trying to put something right; but it is quite clear to all observers, and perhaps to the patient, that there will be no success. We know that Lady Macbeth cannot undo the past and get away from her evil intentions by washing her hands. In obsessional neurosis we sometimes get a ritual which is like a caricature of a religion, as if the God of the religion were dead or temporarily unavailable. Obsessive thinking may be a feature whereby every attempt is made to annul one idea by another, but nothing succeeds. Behind the whole process is a confusion, and no amount of tidying that the patient can do alters this confusion, because it is maintained; it is unconsciously maintained in order to hide something very simple; namely, the fact that, in some specific setting of which the patient is unaware, hate is more powerful than love.

I will cite the case of a girl who could not go to the seaside because she saw in the waves someone crying out for help. Intolerable guilt made her go to absurd lengths in arranging for vigilance and rescue. The absurdity of the symptom could be shown by the fact that she could not tolerate even a picture postcard of the sea coast. If she saw one by chance in a shop-window she would have to find out who took the photograph, because she would see someone drowning, and she would have to organise relief, in spite of the fact that she knew perfectly well that the photograph was taken months and even years previously. This very ill girl was able eventually to come through to a fairly normal life, much less hampered by irrational guilt feeling; but the treatment was necessarily of long duration.

Melancholia is an organised form of the depressed mood to which almost all people are liable. A melancholic patient may be paralysed by a sense of guilt, and may sit for years accusing himself or herself of causing the world war. No argument has any effect whatever. When it is possible to carry out an analysis of such a case, it is found that this gathering into the self of guilt for all the people in the world gives way in the treatment to the patient's fear that hate will be greater than love. The illness is an attempt to do the impossible. The patient absurdly claims responsibility for general disaster, but in so doing avoids reaching his or her personal destructiveness.

A little girl of five reacted with a deep depression to the death of her father which took place in unusual circumstances. The father had bought a car at a time when the little girl was going through a phase in which she was hating her father as well as loving him. She was, in fact, having dreams of his death, and when he proposed a car ride she implored him not to go. He insisted on going, as would be natural since children are liable to these nightmares. The family went for a ride, and it happened that they had an accident; the car was turned over and the little girl was the only one who was uninjured. She went up to her father who was lying in the road and kicked him to wake him up. But he was dead. I was able to watch this child through her serious depressive illness in which she had almost total apathy. For hours she stood in my room and nothing happened. One day she kicked the wall very gently with the same foot that she had used to kick her dead father to wake him up. I was able to put into words her wish to wake her father whom she loved, though in kicking him she was also expressing anger. From that moment of her kicking the wall she gradually came back into life, and after a year or so was able to return to school and to lead a normal life.

It was possible to have an intuitive understanding of unexplained guilt and of obsessional and melancholic illnesses apart from psycho-analysis. It is probably true, however, to say that it is only Freud's instrument of psycho-analysis and its derivatives that have made it possible for us to help the individual who is burdened by guilt-feeling to find the true origin of the sense of guilt in his or her own nature. The sense of guilt, seen this way, is a special form of anxiety associated with ambivalence, or co-existing love and hate. But ambivalence and the toleration of it by the individual implies a considerable degree of growth and health.

2. *Guilt at Its Point of Origin*

I now come to a study of the point of origin of this capacity for guilt-sense, a point which exists in each individual. Melanie Klein (1) drew the attention of psycho-analysts to a very important stage in emotional development to which she gave the name, 'the depressive position'. Her work on the origin of the capacity for guilt-sense in the human individual is an important result of the continued application of Freud's method. It is not possible to do justice to the complexities of the concept of the depressive position in a lecture of this length, but I will attempt a very brief statement.

It should be noted that whereas the earlier work of psycho-analysts dwelt on the conflict between love and hate, especially in the three-body or triangular situation, Melanie Klein more especially has developed the idea of conflict in the simple two-body relationship of the infant to the mother, conflict arising out of the destructive ideas that accompany the love impulse. Naturally, the date of the original version of this stage in an individual's development is earlier than the date of the Oedipus complex.

The accent changes. In previous work the accent was on the satisfaction that the infant obtained from instinctual experience. Now the accent shifts on to the aim, as it gradually appears. When Mrs Klein says that the infant aims at breaking ruthlessly through into the mother to take out of her everything that is felt there to be good, she is not of course denying the simple fact that instinctual experiences yield satisfaction. Nor was the aim altogether neglected in the earlier psycho-analytic formulations. Klein has developed the idea, however, that the primitive love impulse has an aggressive aim; being ruthless, it carries with it a variable quantity of destructive ideas unaffected by concern. These ideas may be very restricted at the beginning, but the infant we are watching and caring for need not be many months old before we can be fairly certain that we can perceive also the beginnings of concern—concern as to the results of the instinctual moments that belong to the developing love of the mother. If the mother behaves in that highly adaptive way which may come naturally to her, she is able to give plenty of time for the infant to come to terms with the fact that the object of the ruthless attack is the mother, the same person who is responsible for the total infant-care situation. It can be seen that the infant has two concerns; one as to the effect of the attack on the mother, and the other as to the results in the infant's own self according to whether there was a predominance of satisfaction or of frustration and anger. (I have used the expression primitive love impulse, but in Klein's writings the reference is to the aggression that is associated with the frustrations that inevitably disturb instinctual satisfactions as the child begins to be affected by the demands of reality.)

A great deal is being assumed here. For instance, we assume that the child is becoming a unit, and is becoming able to perceive the mother as a person. We also assume an ability to bring together the aggressive and erotic instinctual components into a sadistic experience, as well as an ability to find an object at the height of instinctual excitement. All of these developments may go wrong in their earlier stages, those stages which belong to the very beginning of life after birth and which depend on the mother and her natural handling of her infant. When we speak of the origins of guilt-sense, we assume healthy development at earlier stages. At what is called the depressive position the infant is not so much dependent on the mother's simple ability to hold a baby, which was her characteristic at the earlier stages, as on her ability to hold the infant-care situation over a period of time during which the infant may go through complex experiences. If time is given—a few hours maybe— the infant is able to work through the results of an instinctual experience. The mother, being still there, is able to be ready to receive and to understand if the infant has the natural impulse to give or to repair. At this stage in particular the infant is not able to deal with a succession of minders or prolonged absence of the mother. The infant's need for opportunity to make reparation and restitution, if oral sadism is to be accepted by the immature ego, is the second contribution of Klein to this field.

Bowlby has been particularly interested in making the public aware of the need of every small child for a certain degree of reliability and continuity in external relationships. (See Chapter II.) In the seventeenth century Richard Burton listed among the causes of melancholy: 'non-necessary, out-ward, adventitious, or accidental causes: as from the Nurse'. He was thinking partly in terms of the passage of noxious matters from the nurse via the milk, but not entirely so. For instance, he quotes from Aristotle who '. . . would not have a child put to nurse at all, but every mother to bring up her own, of what condition soever she be: . . . the mother will be more careful, loving and attendant, than any servile woman, or such hired creatures; this all the world acknowledgeth. . . .'

The observation of the origin of concern is better made in the analysis of a child or an adult than by direct observa-tion of infants. In formulating these theories we do, of course, need to allow for distortions and sophistications that come from the reporting back that is inherent in the analytic situation. We are able, however, to get a view in our work of this most important development in human individuals, the origin of the capacity for a sense of guilt. Gradually as the infant finds out that the mother survives and accepts the restitutive gesture, so the infant becomes able to accept responsibility for the total phantasy of the full instinctual impulse that was previously ruthless. Ruthlessness gives way to ruth, unconcern to concern. (These terms refer to early development.)

In analysis one could say: 'Couldn't care less' gives way to guilt-feeling. There is a gradual building up towards this point. No more fascinating experience awaits the analyst than the observation of the gradual build-up of the individual's capacity to tolerate the aggressive elements in the primitive love impulse. As I have said, this involves a gradual recognition of the difference between fact and phantasy, and of the mother's capacity to survive the instinctual moment, and so to be there to receive and understand the true reparative gesture.

As will be readily understood, this important phase of development is composed of innumerable repetitions spread over a period of time. There is a benign circle of (i) instinctual experience, (ii) acceptance of responsibility which is called guilt, (iii) a working through, and (iv) a true restitutive gesture. This can be reversed into a malign circle if something goes wrong at any point, in which case we see an undoing of the capacity for a sense of guilt and its replacement by inhibition of instinct or some other primitive form of defence, such as the splitting of objects into good and bad, etc. The question will certainly be asked: at what age in the normal child's development can the capacity for guilt-sense be said to become established? I suggest that we are talking about the first year of the infant's life, and in fact about the whole period in which the infant is having a clearly human two-body relationship with the mother. There is no need to claim that these things happen very early, although possibly they do. By the age of six months an infant can be seen to have a highly complex psychology, and it is possible that the *beginnings* of the depressive position are to be found by this age. There are immense difficulties in fixing the date of the origin of the guilt feelings in the normal infant, and although it is a matter of great interest to seek an answer, the actual work of analysis is not affected by this issue.

There is a great deal in Melanie Klein's further work that I shall not be able to describe in this lecture, although it is relevant. In particular she has enriched our understanding of the complex relationship between phantasy and Freud's concept of inner reality, a concept that was clearly derived from philosophy. Klein has studied the interplay of what is felt by the infant to be benign or malevolent in terms of forces or objects within the self. This third contribution that she has made in this particular field reaches towards the problem of the eternal struggle in man's inner nature. Through the study of the growth of the infant's and the child's inner reality, we get a glimpse of the reason why there exists a relationship between the deepest conflicts that reveal themselves in religion and in art forms and the depressed mood or melancholic illness. At the centre is doubt, doubt as to the outcome of the struggle between the forces of good and evil, or in psychiatric terms, between the benign and persecutory elements within and without the personality. At the depressive position in emotional development of an infant or a patient, we see the building up of the good and bad according to whether the instinctual experiences are satisfactory or frustrative. The good becomes protected from the bad, and a highly complex personal pattern is established as a system of defence against chaos within and without.

From my personal point of view, the work of Klein has enabled psycho-analytic theory to begin to include the idea of an individual's *value*, whereas in early psycho-analysis the statement was in terms of *health* and neurotic *ill-health*. Value is intimately bound up with the capacity for guilt-feeling.

3. *Sense of Guilt Conspicuous by Its Absence*

I have now reached the third part of my lecture, in which I shall first briefly refer to the lack of a moral sense. Undoubtedly, in a proportion of people there is a lack of capacity for guilt-sense. The extreme of this incapacity for concern must be rare. But it is not rare to find individuals who have made a healthy development only in part, and who in part are unable to achieve concern or guilt-feeling, or even remorse. It is tempting here to fall back for an explanation on to the constitutional factor, which of course can never be ignored. However, psycho-analysis offers another explanation. This is that those who lack moral sense have lacked at the early stages of their development the emotional and physical setting which would have enabled a capacity for guilt-sense to have developed.

It should be understood that I am not denying that each infant carries a tendency towards the development of guilt. Given certain conditions of physical health and care, walking and talking appear because the time has come for these developments. In the case of the development of a capacity for guilt-feeling, the necessary environmental conditions are, however, of a much more complex order, comprising indeed all that is natural and reliable in infant and child care. In the earliest stages of the emotional development of the individual, we must not look for a guilt-sense. The ego is not sufficiently strong and organised to accept responsibility for id-impulses, and dependence is near absolute. If there is satisfactory development in the earliest stages, there comes about an ego integration which makes possible the beginning of a capacity for concern. Gradually, in favourable circumstances, a capacity for guilt-sense builds up in the individual in relation to the mother, and this is intimately related to the opportunity for reparation. When the capacity for concern is established, the individual begins to be in a position to experience the Oedipus complex, and to tolerate the ambivalence that is inherent at the later stage in which the child, if mature, is involved in triangular relationships as between whole human beings.

In this context I can do no more than acknowledge the fact that in some persons, or in a part of some persons, there is a stunting of emotional development in the earliest phases, and consequently an absence of moral sense. Where there is lack of personal moral sense the implanted moral code is necessary but the resultant socialisation is unstable.

The Creative Artist

It is interesting to note that the creative artist is able to reach to a kind of socialisation which obviates the need for guilt-feeling and the associated reparative and restitutive activity that forms the basis for ordinary constructive work. The creative artist or thinker may, in fact, fail to understand, or even may despise, the feelings of concern that motivate a less creative person; and of the artist it may be said that some have no capacity for guilt and yet achieve a socialisation through their exceptional talent. Ordinary guilt-ridden people find this bewildering; yet they have a sneaking regard for ruthlessness that does in fact, in such circumstances, achieve more than guilt-driven labour.

Loss and Recovery of Guilt-sense

In our management of antisocial children and adults we can watch the loss or recovery of the capacity for guilt-sense, and often we are in a position to assess the variations in environmental reliability which produce these effects. It is at this point of loss and recovery of moral sense that we can study delinquency and recidivism. Freud (2) wrote in 1915 (referring to adolescent and pre-adolescent acts, such as thefts, frauds, and arson, in people who have eventually become socially adjusted): 'The analytic work . . . afforded the surprising conclusion that such deeds are done precisely *because* they are forbidden, and because by carrying them out the doer enjoys a sense of mental relief, of which he did not know the origin, and after he had committed a misdeed the oppression was mitigated. The sense of guilt was at least in some way accounted for.' Although Freud was referring to late stages in development, what he wrote applies even to children.

From our analytic work we can roughly divide antisocial behaviour into two kinds. The first is common and closely allied to the ordinary naughtiness of healthy children. In terms of behaviour the complaint is of stealing, lying, destructiveness, and bed-wetting. Repeatedly we find that these acts are done in an unconscious attempt to make sense of guilt-feeling. The child or adult cannot reach the source of a sense of guilt that is intolerable, and the fact that the guilt-feeling cannot be explained makes for a feeling of madness. The antisocial person gets relief by devising a limited crime which is only in a disguised way in the nature of the crime in the repressed phantasy that belongs to the original Oedipus complex. This is the closest that the antisocial person can get to the ambivalence belonging to the Oedipus complex. At first the substitute crime or delinquency is unsatisfactory to the delinquent, but when compulsively repeated it acquires the characteristics of secondary gain and thus becomes acceptable to the self. Our treatment is more likely to be effectual when we can apply it before secondary gain has become important. In this, the more common variety of antisocial behaviour, it is not so much the guilt that is repressed as the phantasy that explains the guilt.

By contrast, in the more serious and more rare antisocial episodes it is precisely the capacity for guilt-feeling that is lost. Here we find the most ugly crimes. We see the criminal engaged in a desperate attempt to feel guilty. It is unlikely that he ever succeeds. In order to develop a capacity for guilt-sense, such a person must find an environment of a specialised kind; in fact, we must supply for him an environment that corresponds to that which is normally needed by the immature infant. It is notoriously difficult to provide such an environment, which must be able to take up all the strains resulting from ruthlessness and impulsiveness. We find ourselves dealing with an infant, but one who has the strength and cunning of the older child or adult.

In the management of the more common type of case in which there is antisocial behaviour we are frequently able to produce a cure by rearrangement of the environment, basing what we do on the understanding that Freud has given us.

I shall give an example, that of a boy who was stealing at school. The headmaster, instead of punishing him, recognised that he was ill and recommended psychiatric consultation. This boy at the age of nine was dealing with a deprivation belonging to an earlier age, and what he needed was a period at home. His family had become reunited and this had given him a new hope. I found that the boy had been under a compulsion to steal, hearing a voice that ordered him about, the voice of a wizard. At home he became ill, infantile, dependent, enuretic, apathetic. His parents met his needs and allowed him to be ill. In the end they were rewarded by his making a spontaneous recovery. After a year he was able to return to boarding-school, and the recovery has proved to be a lasting one.

It would have been easy to have diverted this boy from the path that led to his recovery. He was of course unaware of the intolerable loneliness and emptiness that lay at the back of his illness, and which made him adopt the wizard in place of a more natural super-ego organisation; this loneliness belonged to a time of separation from his family when he was five. If he had been thrashed or if the headmaster had told him that he ought to feel wicked, he would have hardened up and organised a fuller identification with the wizard; he would then have become domineering and defiant and eventually an anti-social case. This is a common type of case in child psychiatry, and I choose it simply because it is a published case and reference can be made to it for further details. (3)

We cannot hope to cure many of those who have become delinquent, but we can hope to understand how to prevent the development of the antisocial tendency. We can at least avoid interrupting the developing relationship between mother and baby. Also, applying these principles to the ordinary upbringing of children, we can see the need for some strictness in management where the child's own guilt-sense is still primitive and crude; by limited prohibitions we give opportunity for that limited naughtiness which we call healthy, and which contains much of the child's spontaneity.

More than anyone else it was Freud who paved the way for the understanding of antisocial behaviour and of crime as a *sequel* to an unconscious criminal intention, and a symptom of a failure in child-care. I suggest that in putting forward these ideas and showing how we can test them and use them Freud has made a contribution to social psychology which can have far-reaching results.

BIBLIOGRAPHY

(1) KLEIN, Melanie. *Contributions to Psycho-Analysis. 1921–1945.* London: Hogarth Press, 1948.

(2) FREUD, S., 'Character Types in Psycho-analytic Work,' *Collected Papers*, Vol. 4, p. 342.

(3) WINNICOTT, D. W. (1953). 'Symptom Tolerance in Paediatrics', *Proceedings of the Royal Society of Medicine*, Vol. 46, No. 8, pp. 675–84. 'Section of Paediatrics,' pp. 17–26.

II

PSYCHO-ANALYSIS AND CHILD
CARE

By John Bowlby, m.a., m.d.

Perhaps no other field of contemporary thought shows the influence of Freud's work more clearly than that of child care. Although there had always been those who had known that the child was father to the man and that mother-love gave something indispensable to the growing infant, before Freud these age-old truths had never been the subjects of scientific inquiry; they were therefore readily brushed aside as unvalidated sentimentality. Freud not only insisted on the obvious fact that the roots of our emotional life lie in infancy and early childhood, but also sought to explore in a systematic way the connection between events of early years and the structure and function of later personality.

Although, as we all know, Freud's formulations have met with much opposition—as recently as 1950 eminent psychiatrists were telling us that there was no evidence that what happens in the early years is of relevance to mental health—today many of his basic propositions are taken for granted. Not only do we find popular journals like *Picture Post* telling its public that 'the unhappy child becomes the unhappy neurotic adult' and that what is important is 'the behaviour of those amongst whom a child grows up; . . . and, in the earliest years, especially the behaviour of the mother' (1); but these views are echoed in the publications of Whitehall. The Home Office in describing the work of its Children's Department notes that 'A child's past experiences play a vital part in his development, and continue to be important to him . . .' and advises that 'The aim should be to secure as far as possible that each baby is cared for regularly by the same person'. (2) Finally there is a report

(3) prepared by a committee appointed by the Minister of Education which deals comprehensively with all the problems of the maladjusted child. It bases its recommendations uncompromisingly on such propositions as 'Modern research suggests that the most formative influences are those which the child experiences before he comes to school at all, and that certain attitudes have by then taken shape which may affect decisively the whole of his subsequent development', and 'Whether a child is happy and stable in this period (later childhood), or unhappy and out of step with society or with his lessons, largely depends on one thing—the adequacy of his early nurture'. In celebrating the centenary of the birth of the founder of psycho-analysis it is fitting that we should record this revolution in contemporary thought.

In regard to some at least of the crucial issues of child care there is now much agreement amongst psycho-analysts and those influenced by them. All, for instance, are agreed on the vital importance of a stable and permanent relationship with a loving mother (or mother substitute) throughout infancy and childhood and of the need for awaiting maturation before venturing upon interventions such as weaning and toilet training—and, indeed, on all other steps in the child's 'education'. On other issues, however, there are differences of opinion, and in view of the relative novelty of the scientific study of these problems and their complexity, it would be surprising were there not. This is often confusing and perplexing for parents, especially those 'hot for certainty in this our life'. How much easier it would be for all of us if we knew all or at least a few more of the answers to the problem of how to bring up our children. But this is far from being the position today, and I do not for a moment wish to give the impression that it is. Yet I believe that Freud's work has provided us with some firm knowledge, and, moreover, what perhaps is even more important, shown us a fruitful way of viewing problems of child care and seeking further understanding of them.

Ambivalence and Its Regulation 1616526

Dr. Winnicott, in his lecture on psycho-analysis and guilt
(Chapter I), discussed the vital role in human development
of the growth of a healthy capacity for feeling guilt. He made
it plain that a capacity to experience guilt is a necessary
attribute of the healthy person. Disagreeable though it is,
like physical pain and anxiety, it is biologically indispensable and part of the price we pay for the privilege of being
human beings. Further, he proceeded to describe how the
capacity for feeling guilt 'implies the tolerance of ambivalence' and an acceptance of responsibility for both our love
and our hate. These are themes which, largely due to the
influence of Melanie Klein, have been of major interest to
British analysts. It is my intention tonight to discuss further
the role of ambivalence in psychic life—this inconvenient
tendency we all have to get angry with and sometimes to
hate the very person we most care for—and to consider those
methods of child care which seem to make it easier or more
difficult for a child to grow up capable of regulating this
conflict in a mature and constructive way. For I believe
that a principal criterion for judging the value of different
methods of child care lies in the effects, beneficial or adverse,
which they have on the child's developing capacity to
regulate his conflict of love and hate and, through this, his
capacity to experience in a healthy way his anxiety and
guilt.

Let us briefly trace Freud's ideas on the theme of ambivalence. Of the countless themes running through his work,
none is brighter nor more persistent than this one. It makes
its first appearance in the earliest days of psycho-analysis.
During his investigation of dreams Freud (4) realised that a
dream in which a loved person dies often indicates the
existence of an unconscious wish that that person should
die—a revelation which, if less surprising than when first
advanced, is perhaps no less disturbing today than it was
half a century ago. In his search for the origin of these un-
welcome wishes, Freud turned to the emotional life of

children and advanced what was then the bold hypothesis that in our early years it is the rule and not the exception that towards both our siblings and our parents we are impelled by feelings of anger and hatred as well as those of concern and love. Indeed, it is in this context that Freud first introduced the world to the now familiar themes of sibling rivalry and Oedipal jealousy.

In the few years after the publication of his great work on dreams, Freud's interest in infantile sexuality leads to the theme of ambivalence being less prominent in his writings. It reappears in 1909 when, in a paper on obsessional neurosis, he reminds us that 'in every neurosis we come upon the same suppressed instincts behind the symptoms . . . hatred kept suppressed in the unconscious by love. . . .' (5) A few years later (6) to emphasise the key significance of this conflict, Freud introduced the term ambivalence which had recently been coined by Bleuler.

The clinical significance which Freud attached to ambivalence is reflected in his theoretical constructions. In the earlier of his two major formulations we find him postulating that intra-psychic conflict takes place between the sexual and the ego instincts. Since at the time Freud held that the aggressive impulses were a part of the ego instincts, he is able to sum up by saying that the 'sexual and ego instincts readily develop an antithesis which repeats that of love and hate' (7). The same basic conflict is mirrored again in the second of his formulations—that concerning the conflict between life and death instincts. In this terminology we find that the ambivalence met with in neurotic patients is regarded by Freud as due either to a failure in the process of fusion of the life and death instincts or to a later breakdown of fusion—namely, defusion (8). Once again therefore he sees the crucial clinical and theoretical problem as that of understanding how the conflict between love and hate comes to be regulated satisfactorily or not.

Opinions vary on the merits of these metapsychological formulations of Freud, and will continue to do so for many decades. Sometimes I have wondered whether the theoretical controversies they have stimulated and the abstract language in which they are couched may not have tended to blur the stark nakedness and simplicity of the conflict with which humanity is oppressed—that of getting angry with and wishing to hurt the very person who is most loved. This is a disposition of mankind which has always occupied a central position in Christian theology, and which is well known to us by such colloquial phrases as 'biting the hand that feeds us' and 'killing the goose which lays the golden eggs'. It is the theme of Oscar Wilde's *Ballad of Reading Gaol*, of which one verse runs:

> *Yet each man kills the thing he loves,*
> *By each let this be heard,*
> *Some do it with a bitter look,*
> *Some with a flattering word.*
> *The coward does it with a kiss,*
> *The brave man with a sword!*

It is thanks to Freud that the significance of this conflict in man's life has been realised afresh and thanks to him, too, that it is for the first time the subject of scientific inquiry. We now know that it is the fear and guilt stemming from this conflict which underlies much psychological illness, and the inability to face this fear and guilt which underlies much character disorder, including persistent delinquency. Although our work will take a big step forward when theoretical issues are clearer, for many purposes I believe we can make good progress using such everyday concepts as love and hate, and the conflict—the inevitable conflict—which develops within us when they are directed towards one and the same person.

It will be clear then that the steps by which an infant or child progresses towards the regulation of his ambivalence are of critical import for the development of his personality. If he follows a favourable course, he will grow up not only aware of the existence within himself of contradictory impulses but able to direct and control them, and the anxiety and guilt which they engender will be bearable. If his progress is less favourable, he will be beset by impulses over which he feels he has inadequate or even no control; as a result, he will suffer acute anxiety regarding the safety of the persons he loves and be afraid, too, of the retribution which he believes will fall on his own head. This way lies danger—the danger of the personality resorting to one of a series of manoeuvres each of which creates more difficulties than it solves. For instance, fear of the punishment which is expected to result from hostile acts—and also of course from hostile intents, since it is never easy for the child to distinguish clearly one from the other—frequently leads to more aggression. Thus as often as not we find that an aggressive child is acting on the basis that attack is the best means of defence. Similarly guilt can lead to a compulsive demand for reassurance and demonstrations of love and, when these demands are not met, to further hatred and consequently further guilt. These are the vicious circles which result when the capacity to regulate love and hate develops unfavourably.

Furthermore, when the young child lacks confidence in his ability to control his threatening impulses, there is a risk that unwittingly he will turn to one or more of a multitude of primitive and rather ineffective psychic devices designed to protect his loved objects from damage and himself from the pain of a conflict that seems insoluble by other means. These psychic devices, which include repression of one or both components of the conflict—sometimes hate, sometimes love and sometimes both together—displacement, projection, over-compensation, and many others, have one thing in common: instead of the conflict being brought into the open and dealt with for what it is, all these defence mechanisms are evasions and denials that the conflict exists. Little wonder that they are so inefficient!

Before coming to our main theme—the conditions which in childhood favour or retard the development of the capacity to regulate conflict—I want to emphasise one thing more: there is nothing unhealthy about conflict. Quite the contrary: conflict is the normal state of affairs in all of us. Every day of our lives we discover afresh that if we follow one course of action we have to forgo others which are also desired; we discover, in fact, that we cannot eat our cake and have it too. Every day of our lives therefore we have the task of adjudicating between rival interests within ourselves and of regulating conflicts between irreconcilable impulses. The lower animals have the same problem. Lorenz (9) has described how formerly it was thought that only man was the victim of conflicting impulses, but how it is now known that all animals are constantly beset by impulses which are incompatible with one another, such as attack, flight, and sexual approach.

A pretty example is that of the courting robin. Cock and hen robins are dressed alike—both have red breasts. In the spring the cock robin stakes out a territory for himself and has a propensity to attack all intruders with red breasts. This means that when a potential wife enters his territory his first impulse is to attack her and her first impulse is to flee. Only when she becomes coy are the cock's hostile impulses inhibited and his courtship responses evoked. In the early phases of courtship, therefore, both sexes are in a state of conflict, the male torn between attack and sexual advance and the hen between flirtation and flight.

All recent research in psychology and biology has demonstrated unmistakably that behaviour, whether in the lower organisms or in man himself, is the resultant of an almost continuous conflict of interacting impulses: neither man as a species nor neurotic man as an afflicted sub-group has a monopoly of conflict. What characterises the psychologically ill is their inability satisfactorily to regulate their conflicts.

Conditions which make for Difficulty

What, then, do we know of the conditions which make for difficulty? There can be little doubt that a principal feature of conflict which makes it difficult to regulate is the magnitude of its components. In the case of ambivalence, if either the impulse to obtain libidinal satisfaction or the impulse to hurt and destroy the loved object is unusually strong, the problem of regulating the conflict will be increased. Freud realised this from the beginning. Very early in his work he dismissed the idea that it was either the existence or the nature of the conflicts experienced which distinguished the mentally healthy from those less fortunate; he suggested instead that the difference lay in that psychoneurotics exhibit 'on a magnified scale feelings of love and hatred to their parents which occur less obviously and less intensely in the minds of most children' (10). This is a view which has been abundantly confirmed by clinical work in the past fifty years.

One key to child care is therefore so to treat the child that neither of the two impulses which endanger the loved object —libidinal greed and hatred—will become too intense. Unlike some analysts who are rather pessimistic about the innate strength of the child's impulses, I believe this condition is in most children fairly easily met provided one thing —that the child has loving parents. If the baby and young child has the love and company of his mother and soon also that of his father, he will grow up without an undue pressure of libidinal craving and without an overstrong propensity for hatred. If he does not have these things there is a likelihood that his libidinal craving will be high, which means that he will be constantly seeking love and affection, and constantly prone to hate those who fail, or seem to him to fail, to give it him.

Although the overriding need of the infant and child for love and security is now well-known, there are some who protest against it. Why should the infant make such demands? Why can't he be satisfied with less care and attention? How can we arrange things so that parents have an easier time? Perhaps one day, when we know more about the young child's libidinal needs, we may be able to describe his minimal requirements more precisely. In the meanwhile we should be wise to respect his needs and to realise that to deny them is often to generate in him powerful forces of libidinal demand and propensity to hatred which can later cause great difficulties for both him and us.

Let us not minimise the difficulties for women to which the necessity of meeting the infant's needs give rise. In days gone by, when higher education was closed to them, there was less conflict between the claims of family and career, though the frustration to able and ambitious women was none the less great. Today things are very different. We welcome women into the professions where they have come to play an indispensable part. Indeed, in all fields connected with the health and welfare of children they have been amongst our leaders. Yet this progress, like all growth and development, has brought its tensions, and many of you here tonight will know at first hand the problem of regulating the conflicting demands of family and career. The solution is not easy and it ill-becomes those of us fortunate enough not to be faced with the problem to lay down the law to the other sex how they should resolve it. Let us hope that as time goes on our society, still largely organised to suit men and fathers, will adjust itself to the needs of women and mothers, and that social traditions will be evolved which will guide the individual into a wise course of action.

Let us now return to our theme and consider what happens when, for any reason, the infant's needs are not met sufficiently and at the right time. For some years now I have been interested to inquire into the ill-effects attending the separation of young children from their mothers at a time after they have formed an emotional relationship with them. There have been several reasons for my selecting this as a topic for research: firstly, results have immediate and valuable application; secondly, it is an area in which we can get comparatively firm data and so show those still hypercritical of psycho-analysis that it has good claims to scientific status; finally, the experience of a young child being separated from his mother provides us with a dramatic if tragic example of this central problem of psycho-pathology—the generation of conflict so great that the normal means of its regulation are shattered.

It now seems fairly certain that it is because of the intensity both of libidinal demand and of hatred which are generated that a young child's separation from his mother after he has formed an emotional relationship with her can be so damaging to the development of his personality. For some years we have known of the intense yearning and fretting which so many small children manifest on admission to hospital or residential nursery, and the desperate way in which later, after their feelings have thawed on their return home, they cling to and follow their mothers. The raised intensity of their libidinal demands needs no emphasising. Similarly, we have learnt of the way these children reject their mothers when they first see them again and make bitter accusations against their mothers for deserting them.

Many examples of intense hostility directed against the figure most loved were recorded by Anna Freud and Dorothy Burlingham in the reports of the Hampstead Nurseries during the war. A particularly poignant example is that of Reggie who, except for an interval of two months, had spent all his life in the nurseries since he was five months old. During his stay he had formed 'two passionate relationships to two young nurses who took care of him at different periods. The second attachment was suddenly broken at two years and eight months when his "own" nurse married. He was completely lost and desperate after her departure, and refused to look at her when she visited him a fortnight later. He turned his head to the other side when she spoke to him, but stared at the door, which had closed behind her, after she had left the room. In the evening in bed he sat up and said: "My very own Mary-Ann! But I don't like her" ' (11).

Experiences such as these, especially if repeated, lead to a sense of being unloved, deserted, and rejected. It is these sentiments which are expressed in the tragic-comic poems of an eleven-year-old delinquent boy whose mother had died when he was fifteen months old, and who had thenceforward experienced several substitute mothers. Here is one of the verses (whether original or not I am uncertain) which he wrote during his treatment with my colleague, Yana Popper, which seems to express what he felt to have been the reason for his having been passed from one mother figure to another:

> *Jumbo had a baby dressed in green,*
> *wrapped it up in paper and sent it to the Queen.*
> *The Queen did not like it because it was too fat,*
> *She cut it up in pieces and gave it to the cat.*
> *The cat did not like it because it was too thin,*
> *She cut it up in pieces and gave it to the King.*
> *The King did not like it because he was too slow,*
> *Threw it out the window and gave it to the crow.*

Later, when his therapist was going on holiday he expressed his despair of ever being loved in the words of a traditional ditty:

> *Oh, my little darling, I love you;*
> *Oh, my little darling, I don't believe you do.*
> *If you really loved me, as you say you do,*
> *You would not go to America and leave me at the Zoo.*

It is hardly surprising that such intense despair is coupled with an equally intense hatred. The more he came to care for his therapist the more prone he was to outbreaks of violent hatred, some of which came near to being dangerous. It seemed plain that the repeated separations of his early years had generated in this boy the tendency to intense ambivalence of a magnitude which his immature psychic equipment had been unable to regulate harmoniously, and that the pathological patterns of regulation adopted in his early years had persisted.

Further evidence of the way in which separation from his mother provokes in the young child both intense libidinal need and hatred is provided by a study by my colleague, Christoph Heinicke (12). He compared the responses of two groups of children both aged between fifteen and thirty months; one group were in a residential nursery, the other in a day nursery. Though children of both groups showed a concern to regain their lost parents, those in the residential nursery expressed their desires with far more crying—in other words, more intensely; similarly, it was the children in the residential nursery and not the day nursery children who in various situations were prone to act in a violently hostile way. Though it is only an inference that this hostility is initially directed towards the absent parents, certain findings of this statistically based study are consistent with the hypothesis advanced some years ago (13) that one of the major effects of mother-child separation is a great intensification of the conflict of ambivalence.

So far in considering what it is in early childhood which makes for difficulty in the regulation of ambivalence we have concentrated attention on experiences, such as maternal deprivation, which lead to libidinal craving and hatred running at specially high levels. Naturally there are many other events besides this which can give rise to trouble. Shame and fear, for instance, can make for great difficulties also. Nothing helps a child more than being able to express hostile and jealous feelings candidly, directly, and spontaneously, and there is no parental task more valuable, I believe, than being able to accept with equanimity such expressions of filial piety as 'I hate you, mummy' or 'Daddy you're a beast'. By putting up with these outbursts we show our children that we are not afraid of hatred and that we are confident it can be controlled; moreover, we provide for the child the tolerant atmosphere in which self-control can grow.

Some parents find it difficult to believe that such methods are wise or effective and feel that children should have it impressed on them that hatred and jealousy are not only bad but potentially dangerous. There are two common methods of doing this. One is by the forceful expression of disapproval by means of punishment; the other, more subtle and exploiting his guilt, is by impressing on the child his ingratitude and indicating the pain, physical and moral, which his behaviour causes his devoted parents. Although both methods are intended to control the child's evil passions, clinical experience suggests that neither are very successful and that both exact a heavy toll in unhappiness. Both methods tend to make the child afraid and guilty of his feelings, to drive them underground and so to make it more rather than less difficult for him to control them. Both tend to create difficult personalities, the first—punishment—promoting rebels and, if very severe, delinquents; the second—shame—guilty and anxiety-ridden neurotics. As in politics, so with children: in the long run tolerance of opposition pays handsome dividends.

No doubt much so far will be familiar ground: children need love, security, and tolerance. This is all very well, you may say, but are we never to frustrate our children and are we to let them do just as they please? All this avoidance of frustration, it may be said, will only lead to their growing up to be the barbarian offspring of downtrodden parents. This I believe to be a *non sequitur*; but since these conclusions are so commonly drawn it is worth dealing with them fully.

In the first place the frustrations which really matter are those concerned with the child's need for love and care from his parents. Provided these needs are met, frustrations of other kinds matter little. Not that they are particularly good for him. Indeed, one of the arts of being a good parent lies in the ability to distinguish the avoidable frustrations from the unavoidable. An immense amount of friction and anger in small children and loss of temper on the part of their parents can be avoided by such simple procedures as presenting a legitimate plaything before we intervene to remove his mother's best china, or coaxing him to bed by tactful humouring instead of demanding prompt obedience, or permitting him to select his own diet and to eat it in his own way, including, if he likes it, having a feeding bottle until he is two years of age or over. The amount of fuss and irritation which comes from expecting small children to conform to our own ideas of what, how, and when they should eat is ridiculous and tragic—the more so now that we have so many careful studies demonstrating the efficiency with which babies and young children can regulate their own diets and the convenience to ourselves when we adopt these methods (14).

Granted, however, that there are very many nursery

situations where frustration can be avoided with no inconvenience to ourselves and with beneficial effect on the tempers of all, there are others where it cannot. Fires are dangerous, china is breakable, ink stains the carpet, knives can hurt another child and also hurt the child himself. How do we avoid such catastrophes? The first rule is so to arrange the household that fires are guarded and china, ink, and knives are out of reach. The second is friendly but firm intervention. It is a curious thing how many intelligent adults think that the only alternative to letting a child run wild is to inflict punishment. A policy of firm yet friendly intervention whenever a child is doing something we wish to stop not only creates less bitterness than punishment but in the long run is far more effective. That punishment is efficient as a means of control I believe to be one of the great illusions of Western civilisation. For older children and adults it has its uses as an ancillary to other methods; in the early years I believe it to be out of place both because it is unnecessary and because it can create in anxiety and hatred evils far greater than those it is intended to cure.

Fortunately with babies and young children, who are so much smaller than ourselves, friendly intervention is easy to practise; at a pinch we can pick the child up and carry him bodily away. The price it exacts is our fairly constant presence, a price which I am convinced it is wise for parents to pay. In any case, the notion that young children can be disciplined into obeying rules so that they will toe the line even in our absence is ill-founded. Young children quickly learn what we like and what we dislike, but they have not the necessary psychic apparatus always to carry out our wishes in our absence. Short of terrifying the child into inertia, the disciplining of young children is doomed to failure and those who attempt it to exhausted frustration. As an exemplar of the practice of firm but friendly intervention there is none better than the skilled nursery-school teacher, and from her ways parents can learn much.

It should be noted that this technique of friendly intervention not only avoids stimulating the anger and bitterness albeit unconscious which I believe to be inseparable from punishment, but provides the child with a model for the effective regulation of his conflicts. It shows him that violence, jealousy, and greed can be curbed by peaceful means and that there is no need to resort to those drastic methods of condemnation and punishment which, when copied by the child, are apt to become distorted by his own primitive imagination into pathological guilt and ruthless self-punishment. It is, of course, a technique which is founded on the view which, following Mrs Klein, Dr Winnicott put before us—the view that there is in human beings the germ of an innate morality which, if given the opportunity to grow, provides in the child's personality the emotional foundations of moral behaviour. It is a notion which puts beside the concept of original sin, of which psycho-analysis discovers much evidence in the human heart, the concept of original concern for others or original goodness which, if given favourable circumstances, will gain the upper hand. It is a cautiously optimistic view of human nature, and one which I believe to be justified.

Emotional Problems of Parents

So far we have elaborated some of the conditions of child care which seem likely to promote the healthy development of the capacity to regulate conflict. It is time to consider the problem from the parents' point of view. Are we prescribing, it may well be asked, that parents should be eternally loving, tolerant, and friendlily controlling? I think not . . . and as a parent I hope not. We parents have our angry and jealous feelings too, and whether we like it or not they are going to be expressed sometimes, if not wittingly then unwittingly. It is my belief, and certainly my hope, that if the general background of feeling and relationship is good, the occasional outburst or slap does little harm; it certainly has the advantage of relieving our own feelings, and perhaps also of demonstrating to our children that we have the same problems as they. Such spontaneous expressions of feeling, perhaps with an apology afterwards if we have gone too far, can be distinguished sharply from punishment with its formal assumption of where lie right and wrong. Bernard Shaw's dictum of never hit a child except in hot blood is a good one.

A point which those who are not parents will do well to bear in mind is that it is always far easier to care for other people's children than to care for one's own. Thanks to the emotional bond linking child to parent and parent to child, children always behave in a more babyish way with their parents than with other people. Too often one hears well-meaning people remark that a certain child behaves beautifully with them and that his babyish and difficult behaviour with his mother is due to her foolish management of him: the usual charge is that she spoils him! Such criticisms are usually misplaced and are far more often manifestations of the critic's ignorance of children than of the parent's incompetence. Inevitably the presence of mother or father evokes primitive and turbulent feelings not evoked by other people. This is true even in the bird world. Young finches quite capable of feeding themselves will at once start begging for food in an infantile way if they catch sight of their parents.

Parents then, especially mothers, are much-maligned people; maligned, I fear, particularly by professional workers, medical and non-medical alike. Even so, it would be foolish to pretend we do not make mistakes. Some mistakes are born of ignorance, but perhaps more spring from those unconscious emotional problems which stem from our own childhood. Although when examining children in a child guidance clinic it seems, in a number of cases, that the children's difficulties have arisen through the parents' ignorance of such things as the ill-effects of maternal deprivation or of premature and excessive punishment, far more frequently troubles seem to arise because parents themselves have emotional difficulties of which they are only partially aware and which they cannot control. Sometimes they have read all the latest books on child care and have been to all the lectures of psychologists in the hope that they will discover how to manage their children, but yet things have still gone wrong. Indeed, the failure of many parents with 'psychological ideas' to make a good job of their children has led cynics to decry the ideas. I believe this mistaken. What we must realise, however, is that it is not only what we do but the way that we do it which matters. Feeding on self-demand by an anxious and ambivalent mother will probably lead to far more problems than a routine regulated by the clock in the hands of one who is relaxed and happy. Similarly with modern versus old-fashioned methods of toilet training. This does not mean that the modern methods are not better; it means that they are a part only of what matters and that human beings from infancy onwards are more sensitive to the emotional attitudes of those around them than to anything else.

There is nothing mysterious in this; there is no need to invoke a sixth sense. Very young children are even more alive to the significance of tones of voice, gesture, and facial expression than are adults, and from the first infants are keenly sensitive to the way they are handled.* One very anxious mother whom I am treating has told me how she has discovered that her eighteen months old boy, who she complains is intensely whiny and clinging, responds quite differently according to the way in which she leaves the room. If she jumps up and rushes out to stop the saucepan boiling over, he cries and demands that she returns. If she leaves the room quietly, he hardly notices her departure. In addition to intellectual understanding, which I do not decry, it is from a parent's sensitivity to her child's responses and from her ability to adapt intuitively to his needs that skilled child care is born.

This is nothing new. Time and again we hear it said by teachers and others that a child is suffering because of the attitude of one of his parents, usually the mother. We are told that she is over-anxious or down on the child, over-possessive or rejecting, and time and again such comments are justified. But what the critics have usually failed to take

* See, for instance, the report by Stewart *et al.* (15) on babies who cry excessively. They found this was a response to their mother's difficulties in handling them wisely.

into account is the unconscious origin of these unfavourable attitudes. As a result, all too often the erring parents are subjected to a mixture of exhortation and criticism, each as unhelpful and ineffective as the other.

A psycho-analytic approach at once casts a flood of light on the origin of parents' difficulties and provides a rational way of helping them. Very many of the difficulties encountered by parents, it will not surprise you to learn, stem from their inability to regulate their own ambivalence. When we become parents to a child powerful emotions are evoked, emotions as strong as those which bind the young child to his mother or lovers to one another. In mothers especially there is the same desire for complete possession, the same devotion, and the same withdrawal of interest from others. But, unfortunately, coupled with these delicious and loving feelings there comes all too often an admixture—I hesitate to say it—an admixture of resentment and even of hatred. The intrusion of hostility into the mother's, or the father's, feelings for the baby seems so strange and often so horrifying that some of you may find it difficult to believe. Yet it is a reality, and sometimes a grim reality, both for the parent and the child. What is its origin?

Though it is still difficult to explain this hostility, it seems plain that the feelings which are evoked in us when we become parents have a very great deal in common with the feelings which were evoked in us as children by our parents and siblings. The parent who suffered deprivation may, if she has not become incapable of feeling affection, experience an intense need to possess her child's love, and may go to great lengths to ensure that she obtains it. The parent who was jealous of a younger sibling may come to experience unreasonable hostility to the new 'little stranger' in the family, a sentiment which is particularly common in fathers. The parent whose love for his mother was shot through with antagonism for her demanding ways may come to resent and hate the demanding ways of the infant.

I believe that the trouble does not lie in the simple recurrence of old feelings—perhaps a measure of such feelings is present in every parent—but in the parent's inability to tolerate and to regulate these feelings. Those who in childhood have experienced intense ambivalence towards parents or siblings, and who have then unconsciously resorted to one of the many primitive and precarious means of resolving conflict of which I spoke earlier—repression, displacement, projection, and so on—are unprepared for the renewal of conflict when they come to be parents. Instead of recognising the true nature of their feelings towards the child and adjusting their behaviour accordingly, they find themselves actuated by forces they know not of and are perplexed at being unable to be as loving and patient as they wish. Their difficulty is that the re-emergence of ambivalent feelings is being dealt with, without their knowledge, by the same primitive and precarious methods to which they resorted in their early childhood at a time of life when they had no better methods available. Thus the mother who is constantly apprehensive that her baby may die is unaware of the impulse in herself to kill it and, adopting the same solution she adopted in childhood perhaps in regard to her death-wishes against her own mother, struggles endlessly and fruitlessly to stave off dangers from elsewhere—accidents, illnesses, the carelessness of neighbours. The father who resents the baby's monopoly of the mother and insists to his wife that her attentions are bad for it is unaware that he is motivated by the same kind of jealousy as he experienced in childhood when a younger sibling was born. The same is true of the mother impelled to possess her child's love who, by her endless self-sacrifice, tries to ensure that the child is given no excuse for any feelings other than those of love and gratitude. This mother, who at first sight appears so loving, inevitably creates great resentment in her child by her demands for his love, and equally great guilt in him through her claims to be so good a mother that no sentiment but gratitude is justified. In behaving in this way she is of course not aware that she is seeking from her child the love, and the assurance that she is worthy of love, which she never had when she was small.

I want to repeat that in my view it is not simply that parents are motivated in these ways which creates the difficulties for the children; what makes for trouble is the parents' ignorance of their own motives and their unwitting resort to repression, rationalisation, and projection to deal with their conflicts.

There is probably nothing more damaging to a relationship than when one party attributes his own faults to the other, making him a scapegoat. Unfortunately babies and young children make perfect scapegoats since they manifest so nakedly all the sins that flesh is heir to: they are selfish, jealous, sexy, dirty, and given to tempers, obstinacy, and greed. A parent who carries a load of guilt in regard to one or other of these failings is apt to become unreasoningly intolerant of its manifestations in his child. He torments the child by his vain attempts to eradicate the vice. I recall a father who, troubled all his life by masturbation, tried to stop it in his son by putting him under a cold tap every time he found him with his hand on his genital. By acting in ways such as this the parent intensifies the child's guilt and also his fear and hatred of authority. Some of the most poisoned of parent-child relationships which lead to grave problems in the children stem from parents seeing motes in their children's eyes to avoid seeing beams in their own.

No one with an analytic orientation who has worked in a child guidance clinic can have failed to be impressed by the frequency with which these and comparable emotional problems occur in the parents of children who are referred, or the extent to which the parents' problems seem to have created or exacerbated the children's difficulties. Indeed, they are so frequent that in many clinics as much attention is given to helping the parents solve their emotional problems as to helping the children with theirs. It is therefore curious to reflect that this is an aspect of psychological illness which seems to have been almost unknown to Freud, and, perhaps for this reason, one to which psycho-analysts have, in my view, still to give proper attention. Yet it is one which I believe to be pregnant with hope for the future. Such limited experience as we have suggests that skilled help given to parents in the critical months before and after childbirth and in the early years of a child's life may go far in assisting them to develop the affectionate and understanding relationship to the baby which almost all of them desire. We know that the infant's earliest years when, unknown to him, the foundations of his personality are being laid are a critical period in his development. In the same way it seems that the early months and years after a baby is born are a critical period in the development of a mother and a father. In this earliest phase of parenthood parents' feelings seem more accessible than at other times, help is often both sought and welcomed and, because the relationships in the family are still plastic, it is effective. Relatively little help, if skilled and given at this time, may thus go a long way. If we are right in thinking this, then the family with a new baby is a strategic point at which to tackle the malign circle of disturbed children growing up to become disturbed parents who in turn handle their children in such a way that the next generation develops the same or similar troubles. The advantage of treating children young is now well-known; we are now advocating that parents, too, should be helped soon after they are 'born'!

The recognition that a principal cause of parental mistakes lies in the feeling which they have for their children being distorted by unconscious conflicts stemming from their own childhood is one which perhaps has not yet been absorbed into contemporary thought. Not only is it disturbing and alarming to parents, many of whom not unnaturally hope to see the family difficulty elsewhere than in their own hearts, but it is baffling to professional workers, medical and non-medical, to discover that so many of the problems which they face lie in a seemingly intangible realm, of which they have no knowledge and to help in which they have no training. None the less, it is plain that this is so and, if parents are to receive the insightful help which will enable them to become the good parents they seek to be, a much greater understanding of unconscious conflict and its role in creating disturbances in the parents' management of their children will have to be achieved by professional personnel. This poses a problem of the first magnitude, and one too big for us to consider this evening.

Extra-psychic Conflict and Intra-psychic Conflict

The point of view which I am advocating, it will be seen, is based on the belief that much mental ill-health and unhappiness is due to environmental influences which it is in our power to change. In psycho-analysis as in other branches of psychiatry, indeed in all the biological sciences, the contributions respectively of nature and nurture are constantly debated. Our problem is to understand why it is that one individual grows up without great difficulties in his impulse life whilst another is beset by them. There can be no doubt that variations in hereditary endowment and in the influence of environment both play large parts. Freud himself, however, perhaps because his first environmental hypothesis (that regarding the influence of childhood seduction) proved mistaken, was cautious in implicating variations in the environment to account for the difficulties of his patients, and as he grew older seems increasingly to have believed that little could be done by environmental change to mitigate the force of infantile conflict. Many analysts have followed him in this view. Some, indeed, have not only held that those of us who are more hopeful are mistaken but have had misgivings lest by emphasising the significance of environment we divert attention from the crucial fact of intra-psychic conflict. It must be admitted that this danger exists and that books have been written by analysts about child care which have had as their principal focus extra-psychic conflict—namely, the conflict between the child's needs and the limited opportunities provided for their satisfaction by the environment. Although, as I have already indicated, I believe this extra-psychic conflict between inner needs and external opportunity for fulfilling them to be real enough, I want to emphasise that in my view this by itself is of only limited significance for psychic development. What matters about the external environment is the extent to which the frustrations and other influences it imposes lead to the development of *intra*-psychic conflict of a form and intensity such that the immature psychic apparatus of the infant and young child cannot satisfactorily regulate it. It is by this criterion that we should assess the merits or demerits of child-care practices, and it is in approaching the problem in this way, I believe, that psycho-analysis has its principal contribution to make.

Confirmed, indeed enthusiastic, subscriber though I am to the view that the actual situations which the infant or young child experiences are of crucial significance for his development, I repeat that I do not wish to give the impression that we now know how to enable all children to grow up without emotional disturbance. Certainly I believe we already know a good deal, and that, if we were able to apply our present knowledge (and owing to the shortage of trained workers I fear this is a very big 'if'), a tremendous increase in human happiness and a tremendous reduction in psychological illness would follow. Nevertheless, it would be foolish to suppose our knowledge is already such that we can guarantee that if a child has such and such experiences he will grow up without major difficulties. Not only are there such awkward problems to contend with as those arising from the distorting effect of the child's phantasies and his mistaken interpretation of the world around him, about which I have said nothing this evening, but there may well be difficulties of the origins of which at the present time we know nothing whatever. Even about those of which we have some understanding our knowledge is still scanty and insufficiently based on systematically collected data. The need for research is therefore great, and as our understanding increases the opportunities for fruitful research expand.

Which research approaches will prove most fruitful only the future will reveal. All research is a gamble and we have to put our money on the horses we happen to fancy. Out of a big field my own inclination leads me to back cross-breds. It seems to me likely that studies of motivation in young children, especially the study of the way in which the mother and infant develop their highly charged relationship which is of such central concern to psycho-analysis, will gain greatly in precision and clarity from the application of concepts and research methods derived from the European school of animal-behaviour studies, headed by Lorenz and Tinbergen and often known as ethology. Equally I suspect that our insight into the cognitive world which the infant and young child builds for himself, and then inhabits and finally moulds, will be greatly advanced by the concepts and research methods pioneered by Piaget. Similarly, learning theory may be expected to throw light on the learning processes which occur in the critical months and years when a new personality is born. Nevertheless, indispensable though I believe contributions of these kinds will be, they will be barren if they are not constantly interpreted in the light of knowledge gained by intimate contact with the emotional lives of children and parents in a clinical setting, using methods such as those introduced by Melanie Klein and Anna Freud and other child analysts and drawing their ultimate inspiration from the man the centenary of whose birth we celebrate this weeek.

BIBLIOGRAPHY

(1) 'Unhappiness Begins at Home,' *Picture Post.* December 31st, 1955.
(2) *Seventh Report on the Work of the Children's Department.* H.M.S.O., 1955.
(3) *Report of the Committee on Maladjusted Children.* H.M.S.O., 1955.
(4) FREUD, S. (1900), *The Interpretation of Dreams*, Standard Edition IV, pp. 248–64.
(5) FREUD, S. (1909), 'A Case of Obsessional Neurosis', *Collected Papers, III.*
(6) FREUD, S. (1912), 'The Dynamics of the Transference', *Collected Papers, II.*

(7) FREUD, S. (1915), 'Instincts and Their Vicissitudes', *Collected Papers, IV*.

(8) FREUD, S. (1923), *The Ego and the Id*. London: Hogarth Press.

(9) *Discussions on Child Development*, Vol. I, ed. Tanner, J. M., and Inhelder, B. Proceedings of the First Meeting of the World Health Organisation Study Group on Psychobiological Development of the Child. London: Tavistock Publications, 1956.

(10) FREUD, S. (1900), *The Interpretation of Dreams*, Standard Edition IV, p. 261.

(11) BURLINGHAM, D., and FREUD, A. (1944), *Infants without Families*. London: Allen & Unwin.

(12) HEINICKE, C. (1956), 'Some Effects of Separating Two-year-old Children from their Parents: A Comparative Study', *Human Relations*, Vol. 9, No. 2.

(13) BOWLBY, J. (1946), *Forty-four Juvenile Thieves: Their Characters and Home Life*. London: Baillière, Tindall & Cox.

(14) DAVIS, C. M. (1939), 'Results of the Self-selection of Diets by Young Children', *Canad. Med. Assoc. J.*, 41, pp. 257–61.

(15) STEWART et al. (1954), *Amer. J. Psychiatry*, 110, pp. 687–94.

III

PSYCHO-ANALYSIS AND THE TEACHER

By Ilse Hellman, ph.d.

When in this lecture I try to show the part psycho-analysis can play for the teacher, it will not be done with the conviction that knowledge of psycho-analytic theory is indispensable for good teaching. There have been wonderful teachers throughout the ages, and there are wonderful teachers today, who have no knowledge of psycho-analysis; just as there have been parents at all times who were able to give their children what they needed without having to learn about their needs first. Equally, progress in educational theory and practice has taken place long before the age of psycho-analysis. Right through the history of education the process can be traced which has slowly led to the view that the teacher's work is not confined to imparting knowledge of certain facts and skills. All of the famous educators of the past, however differently they may have approached the task or expressed themselves, have had the aim of convincing teachers that the child himself must be the centre of the educational process.

To choose one example, John Dewey, a contemporary of Freud, made it his aim to convince teachers of the importance of studying the development of human beings and to show the important task the school has to play in this developmental process. In the face of much opposition, he gradually came to convince many of the soundness of his approach; and under his influence the greatest strides were made in our understanding that, in order to be successful, teaching must be planned around the child and his interests. Although it was not Dewey's aim to explore the deeper layers of the mind, his approach, which he arrived at independently through different avenues from psycho-analysis, tallies in most of its practical applications with psycho-analytic views on education.

There can be no doubt, however, that psycho-analysis has greatly influenced educational thought since its findings were known—not essentially through the direct application of its theories to teaching, but through the fact that psycho-analysis makes a study of human beings, their development, the forces within them, and their relations with each other. In this way also it has been able to throw light on the very elements of the processes of learning and teaching.

It seems important here to point out that the special contribution psycho-analysis has made to the understanding of human beings rests on the fact that it approaches the study of their behaviour simultaneously from different angles. This has been clearly formulated by Hartmann and Kris (1) in their paper, 'The Genetic Approach in Psycho-Analysis', where they say: 'The reference to psycho-analysis as a genetic psychology is misleading, where it is assumed that its main concern is to trace back behaviour to earlier situations.' It is equally misleading to refer to psycho-analysis as a dynamic psychology only. Psycho-analysis is distinguished from other approaches to the study of human beings by the very fact that it approaches the study of human behaviour from three angles—the genetic, historical, and the dynamic, and by its aim of finding *causal* connections between them. It not only states the fact that in a certain situation the individual repeatedly reacts in the same way, but it tries to explain *why* he is forced to do so. And it not only reveals the situations where similar behaviour was displayed, but traces the way back to earlier situations where different behaviour was at least attempted, and to the failure of these attempts. It is through this approach that psycho-analysis can make its contribution to education; it enables the teacher to look at the child with greater understanding, linking together past, present, and future.

Teachers have often said to me: 'I find it terribly interesting to learn to see children from the psycho-analytic point of view, but isn't it, in fact, discouraging for the teacher?

One is either told that everything of importance has taken place long before the child ever gets to school, or that what can be done for him can only be done by the child analyst.' Or in less friendly terms, as one man put it, 'What good does it do me to be told what the kid has been feeling when he was three months old if I have to cope with him tomorrow?'

Our main questions may then be put in the following terms: can psycho-analysis be more to the teacher than an interesting scientific study? Does the fact that it shows that the foundations of personality are laid in the child's early relations with his parents leave no scope for the teacher's work? And where do the areas lie in which he can feel that he can get personal gain for his work from it?

Freud made no direct formulations concerning education. In his *Autobiographical Study* (2) he says: 'I have contributed nothing to the application of psycho-analysis to education, but it was understandable that the investigations of the sexual life of children and of their psychological development have attracted the attention of educationists and have shown them their task in a new light.'

What then is the new light Freud's findings about the sexual life of children and their development has thrown on the teacher's task? The teacher who enters upon his career today brings with him and finds a multitude of ideas accepted by his teachers, his colleagues, and the children's parents which no longer have the label of psycho-analysis attached to them but which can be traced back to Freud's findings. To take only two of the best known: Most people now accept it as a fact that small children get enjoyment from playing with water and sticky things. Every nursery school provides the chance for it by offering sand and water, plasticine and clay, and teachers know that children will make use of these materials with great impetus and gradually use them for making things rather than just for smearing. The other equally widely accepted fact is that small children are not just delighted when a new baby arrives in the family, but that they have angry feelings as well, which they should be allowed to express.This knowledge has penetrated far—even into the columns of women's weekly papers.

Both of these examples contain fundamental ideas of psycho-analysis; firstly, that there are urges within the child that have to be acknowledged and respected, and that they can be gradually transformed; secondly, that there are conflicting emotions within him, emotions of love and hate, the ambivalence Dr. Bowlby discussed in his paper. These are two examples of new light thrown on children and education that are of far-reaching importance.

Formerly childhood was seen as a phase of innocence and happiness, and it was the aim to maintain this state until maturity. Where manifestations of instincts and intense negative feelings were shown, they were treated as danger signs and were fought and suppressed by strict prohibition. In this light it seems correct to say that psycho-analysis has revolutionised the approach to children and consequently to education. The intense shock Freud's findings produced early on is well known; the resistance against the facts of the unconscious and of infantile sexuality in particular made the acceptance of psycho-analysis slow—and impossible for many. The process was not speeded up by the first experiments at direct application of his findings by parents and educators; they had hoped that by removing, as far as possible, from the child's life external prohibitions which lead to fears and conflicts, the path could be found to the avoidance of neurosis. Freedom for satisfaction of the child's urgent wishes was advocated, irrespective of their nature and of the child's age. Greed, dirtiness, and overt sexual behaviour were given free reign by these experimenters. Authority was done away with to a large extent. Grown-ups attempted to tolerate the children's behaviour with a minimum of intervention. It is not surprising that the results were most disappointing. The children were anxious, unable to bear tension, unable to find satisfaction in pursuits demanding effort. The external world represented by the educator provided too little help in the difficult task of mastering their urges and in the anxiety aroused by them.

Freud himself did not long maintain ideas that could justify such measures. His further formulations concerning neurosis, his work on the structure of the mind (the id, ego, and super-ego), his recognition of the role of aggression and his later views on anxiety, all show clearly that gratification of instincts, irrespective of their nature and of the child's age, and absence of guidance by the teacher cannot lead to mental health. Occasionally we still meet a parent or an educator who tries to act on these assumptions. The idea that the school child is best left alone, that he knows best what he needs and that the grown-up's intervention will only do damage, is outdated. It was once expressed in the story about the visitor to a school of this kind who, asking the children what they were mostly occupied with, got the answer: 'Lie about and develop.'

Isolated examples of extreme misunderstanding do not do justice to the part played by experiments in progressive education. These experiments, in fact, in their courageous exploration have done much to influence the state school system we have in this country today. They are ignored only by those who feel that keeping to tradition is an aim in itself. They may, however, focus attention on the discrepancy which has long existed between popular ideas of psycho-analytically oriented education and the approach psycho-analytic knowledge really brings to education. Two well-known experiments carried out by psycho-analysts themselves in this country, Susan Isaacs' Malting House School in Cambridge thirty years ago (3) and Anna Freud's Hampstead Nurseries opened during the war (4), have brought most valuable insight into these problems, and have shown how at every step in his development his changing relations with the grown-ups help to strengthen the child's weak ego.

Freud has given a vivid description of the situation between the weak ego—the internal mediator who feels his task too great—and the impulses which threaten it by their strength and arouse intolerable anxiety. He used the picture of a rider—comparing the ego to the rider, the impulse to the horse. The rider utilises the horse's strength and power, but riding becomes useful and pleasurable only if the rider is capable of controlling and directing the horse. If the ego is a poor rider, the horse will gallop away, carrying him into danger. Not the rider but the horse is then the master.

The need for the adult as model, as external super-ego, who does not act through fear, but by his friendly, firm intervention, as Dr. Bowlby termed it, while the child is as yet unable to control his passions from within, has been expressed by all psycho-analysts who have themselves worked with children. It was discussed by Susan Isaacs in relation to aggression in the children in her school in the following way:

She says: 'At first I was too passive in my treatment of situations of bullying and cruelty in the hope that if the bullying elders were not interfered with the impulse would die a natural death. But I found this did not happen. And that—I felt sure—was not only because the children were aggressively treated in their own homes, but because the impulse feeds upon itself rather than exhausts itself in fulfilment. When I ceased to remain passive and showed my disapproval, it was not only the younger children who were now saved from teasing, but also the elder, stronger children became more contented. They now felt safeguarded against their own impulses.'

Slow modification, not sudden suppression or total lack of support, is felt to be the educator's task.

The first group of teachers to accept findings of psycho-analysis and put them into practice in a fruitful way were nursery-school teachers. In their daily contacts with pre-school children they do not find it difficult to observe the very passions and the anxiety aroused by the inner conflicts psycho-analysis has pointed out. Anxiety and instinctive urges are openly displayed, and methods of dealing with them can be clearly seen if one has learnt to observe in detail. Phantasies are expressed in play and talk, and the teacher feels she has access to the child's mind. She can learn to evaluate the effect of immediate experiences on the child, and watch the ways his mind can use to deal with them. When teaching, it is not difficult to demonstrate to her some of the main manoeuvres of the mind, *the mechanisms of defence* as we refer to them, and she has a unique chance to see the great variety of ways in which a situation which is similar externally is dealt with by different children. Each morning she can watch them leave their mothers, and their activities and play will give her insight into the ways their egos use to lessen the anxiety aroused by being left; she will, for instance, see one girl turn away quickly and soon get busy with a pram and dolls, caring for them in a loving way. She has, on losing mother's presence, become a mother herself, she has *identified* with her and can now bear her absence. Another child may start a game of hide-and-seek; he wants the teacher to find him, to show distress that he has gone and show delight at his return. It is no longer he who experiences the loss, but she, and he finds relief in feeling that he is in control and can return at will, while really he suffers from his utter helplessness in his need to bring back the mother. He has turned the passive experience into an active one. The teacher also gets to know the meaning of *regression*, the way of dealing with great anxiety by a return to early ways of comfort, by really needing to be held by the teacher or, failing this, by supplying the needed comfort himself through his own body, by sucking, rocking, and withdrawal into phantasy. Knowledge of these and other ways at the disposal of the mind, as Anna Freud has described them in her book *The Ego and the Mechanisms of Defence* (5) are of great help to teachers when they meet such variety of child behaviour, and it can give the lead in knowing how to meet the child's needs, which steps to take in providing the opportunities in school the child can best make use of at a given time.

For the teacher who has no experience of young children, who works with the child in the latency period, as Freud has termed it, access to these internal happenings is not possible in the same way. Defensive measures have come to hide conflicts, and the instinctive urges in their original form are changed, at times, beyond recognition. The teacher shakes his head and finds our description of internal happenings wildly exaggerated; but he can more readily learn to trace the present manifestations back to their earlier sources where the child's interests and activities are concerned, and use them to make the link of past, present, and future in his teaching, knowing that *displacement* of satisfaction is possible and must be used if learning is to bring success.

With adolescents, where conflict of emotions and conflicting tendencies are once more near the surface, the teacher who has become familiar with the young child's struggle, recognises much that is revived. Also, with maladjusted and delinquent children, teachers and probation officers do not find it difficult to see and understand manifestations of behaviour in the light of the unconscious processes which psycho-analysis has shown.

In education too—as in child care—findings of psycho-analysis have been given recognition in official documents. The extent to which this point of view has gained ground in the last decades is clearly shown in publications such as the *Report of the Consultative Committee on Primary Schools*, published by the Board of Education in 1939, and in all recommendations for teachers published by the Ministry of Education since. I am thinking in particular of the recent report on maladjustment (6).

Freedom of Expression, Activity, and *Creativity* are the concepts on which these recommendations are based. Each of these words refers to the existence of forces within the child. It is seen as the teacher's task to provide a setting where they can find expression and be utilised in the process of development of the whole personality, and in acquiring knowledge about the external world.

The realisation that the child's learning is closely bound up with his relationship to the teacher and is an integral part of it follows from our understanding of his earlier needs in relation to his parents. This is thrown into relief by Freud's own account of his feelings about his teachers at school; in an article entitled, 'Some Reflections on Schoolboy Psychology' (7), which he wrote on the occasion of the fiftieth anniversary of his old school, Freud says: 'It is hard to decide whether what affected us more and was of greater importance to us was our concern with the sciences that we were taught or with the personalities of our teachers. It is true, at least, that this second concern was a perpetual undercurrent in all of us, and that in many of us the path to the sciences led only through our teachers. Some of us stopped half-way along that path, and for a few—why not admit as much?—it was on that account blocked for good and all.' He then describes most vividly the intense conflicting emotions he and his fellow students experienced in relation to their teachers; their readiness to love them, which he feels not all of them may have sensed; the boys' intense hatred alternating with love; the search for the teachers' weaknesses, and simultaneously their pride in discovering that they had good qualities and great knowledge.

Freud here looks back on to his own school-days in the light of his discoveries. He attributes a central part to the teacher as the one who can 'open or close the road to knowledge and to the enjoyment of it'. He refers to the fact that intense emotion is a serious obstacle to learning. We all know from experience that states such as being in love, being angry, or anxious are no help in our work!

The teacher's concern has always been to bring about a situation in the classroom which he considers best for teaching and for the pupils' task of learning. Teachers have always been aware of the need to keep out disturbing influences which hinder work. But looking at the measures used to achieve this desired state, we find that they were all directed against the external world—disturbances coming from within were ignored. Restriction of movement and speech were meant to create the condition where attention could best be used for work. Psycho-analysis has shown, however, that the opposite is true; where frustration is imposed and ways of discharge blocked, tension rises, but not *attention*. Discharge is sought in phantasy, through auto-erotic satisfaction, and reality with its interests and demands recedes into the background. The teacher's well-known complaints that the pupils are 'dreaming or fidgeting' belong to this method of trying to increase concentration. Similar examples of confusion between inner and outer world and the part they play in the child's life can be found in other places in traditional educational practice.

Modern teachers have found out that to be able 'to hear a pin drop' is not a basic condition for good work. They have achieved much by opening up the two essential paths of discharge of tension, free movement, and speech, which are the paths of spontaneous expression, communication, and creativity as well. Whoever has seen an 'activity' class at work knows what energy and impetus goes into work, and how the free exchange of ideas between child and teacher contributes to creation of new ideas and knowledge.

But to return to Freud's paper once more, and with it to the question of disturbance from within. He points out two ways in which intense emotion finds entry into the classroom, and thus becomes an obstacle to learning: the *real* features and behaviour of the teacher, and feelings of ambivalence within the child which he brings from his home environment and from his phantasies relating to it, which he *transfers* on to the teacher and his fellow pupils.

It is commonly known that the child reacts to the teacher as a substitute parent. The gain for the child in his adaptation to reality lies in the fact that the teacher does not behave as a parent, does not meet him with intense emotion, but fulfils his demands in new and different ways, more remote from his primitive needs. The teacher enables the child to substitute new satisfactions for these needs by giving him opportunities to learn about and master more and more things in his surroundings. The teacher who by his personality and behaviour lends himself to the role of ideal or feared parent, who evokes intense emotions, revives earlier conflicts at the very time when the school child needs to detach himself from them and to turn towards the external world. The teacher can open the path to work and knowledge if he senses the pupil's wish for proofs that he values him and his efforts, and responds to the child's expectation that he can provide for his needs through his capacity and readiness to give both love and knowledge. Or he may block the path by arousing in the child fear and hatred of him, and through this of the knowledge he is expected to acquire.

Freud gives an example of the way a teacher's attacking behaviour revived a boy's early dread of being attacked and damaged in his paper 'From the History of an Infantile Neurosis' (8) (commonly known as the Wolf-man). As a result of this experience, the boy's capacity to learn the subject this teacher was teaching became inhibited. His early childhood's fear of wolves was suddenly intense again, and the matter was not helped by the fact that the teacher's name was Mr Wolf.

As Susan Isaacs put it: 'The teacher cannot do her work well unless she attracts to herself mainly the forces of love. She must provide generous opportunity for expression of the impulses of destruction, but in a very modified form; for instance, in the rivalry of games, sports, and handiwork. But she must not by her real qualities attract to herself the negative, explosive forces of hatred and aggression.' And then she adds—carefully—in a footnote so teachers should not get frightened and think they were expected to be saints: 'I do not mean that educators have to be inhumanly perfect before they can educate at all. Children readily forgive occasional outbursts of anger, and other real faults in an adult whose general attitude is reliable, friendly, and understanding.'

A small illustration of how a teacher's attitude can keep open or close an avenue of work, and a feeling that the effort is valued or disregarded, came my way the other day. A small girl of my acquaintance proudly returned from school with a strange-looking contraption she had made from old boxes and a cotton-reel and painted in bright colours—it was obviously a house that hadn't quite come off. When asked about it, she said, beamingly: 'Teacher said it's a *beautiful* abstract and tomorrow I'll make another more beautiful still.' I was reminded of my teacher when at that age I drew a house. He crossed it out and said angrily: 'The walls are

crooked, and a chimney like this would fall off immediately.'
It is clear that after four years with him this avenue was
blocked.

The teacher's real behaviour and personality form the
centre of the setting in which good learning can take place,
but in his class he will find that what he *really* is and does
by no means elicits the same reaction from all his pupils.
The role of transference to which Freud refers in his article
on Schoolboy Psychology plays an important part in the
pupil's relations to his teachers.

Awareness of this phenomenon and the part it may play
in the classroom can help teachers to understand and meet
the often baffling, irrational manifestations of behaviour
shown by their pupils, in which the teachers find themselves
the centre of love, idealisation, fear and hatred, ridicule and
envy of single individuals and groups—in no way related
to the real situation.

Although basic differences exist between the relationship
of the child to his teacher and the patient to his analyst,
valuable insight has been gained for the learning situation
from the analytic situation. In his clinical work, Freud discovered that a relationship invariably develops between
patient and analyst in which the patient experiences and
manifests feelings about him and builds up phantasies
around him which he transfers on to him from his parents
and other members of his family circle; or the patient may
see in his analyst certain aspects of his own personality
which he has projected on to him.

In her paper, 'Certain Types and Stages of Social
Maladjustment' (9), Anna Freud gives an illuminating
account of the dangers for favourable adjustment to reality
brought about by continued transference of the family
situation, and of phantasies. She describes what she terms
'a normal stage of social maladjustment' in the young child
who leaves the family circle for the first time and tends to
approach the strange world of people and things on the
basis of his expectations and phantasies built up in the home.

Through primitive defences, such as introjection and

projection, the infantile mind tries to deal with anxiety, and the small child misinterprets and distorts the external world of people and things. He gives them magic qualities, views new people as potentially dangerous, or may approach them all with great expectations and indiscriminate signs of affection. He may interpret anyone's demands made on him as acts of deliberate hostility if he himself feels guilty of hostility. Nursery workers know well that they have to deal with puzzling behaviour of small children. They also know that they can count with most of them on a considerable change as time goes on. We say: the children have got to know the new people and place. This means that they have been able to replace their earlier phantastic attitude by a new one that has become established in their mind through their capacity to 'take in' new real facts and to react to them accordingly.

Where this capacity is disturbed or does not develop at the usual time, children may continue to behave in ways which are not in keeping with reality throughout their school life. Where this is extreme, we refer to them as maladjusted children. This maladjustment, though it may be more apparent in the social realm, has an important bearing also on their learning.

Every classroom contains examples of this nature to a greater or lesser degree. Of these I shall name only two. (i) The pupil who brings to the classroom the phantasy that he is everyone's victim and behaves in such a way that his attempt at provoking criticism or punishment is clear. Through his behaviour such a boy or girl soon becomes the scapegoat of the class and thus gets confirmation of his phantasy that he is victimised, and simultaneously satisfaction for his passive, masochistic wishes. (ii) Another type equally well known, though often considered a real asset to the class, is the 'born monitor' who spends his time keeping others to rules, showing stern disapproval of their behaviour, eventually punishing them or bringing about their punishment by the teacher. He, too, acts under the pressure of one of the 'manoeuvres of the mind', which compels him to look for misdeeds in others, getting satisfaction of his own sense of guilt and of his sadistic impulses in seeing that 'justice is done'.

In the extreme case of such behaviour the teacher who expressed his fear of disappointment to me earlier on is right. He cannot fundamentally alter the internal conditions which compel these children to act as they do; for this he will have to seek expert help. But the importance of his role lies in the fact that he can, by his knowledge of these mechanisms and his insight, prevent himself from responding to the child's provocation and thus join the line of those who confirm his phantasy. The parent's attitude has played its part in producing the child's need to live under the domination of such phantasies, the teacher's different approach helps him to make new and different features part of himself. We speak of *identification* with the teacher, a process of greatest importance in both the formation of the child's personality and his learning in the academic sense.

Identification is an unconscious process and sometimes confused with the deliberate attempts to model oneself superficially after a real person in one's life, or a hero of a far remote period in history or on the screen. Identification is at the basis of learning from the earliest learning of the baby with his mother; all through life 'intake' of something new into the personality plays a decisive part. Where learning was concerned, we have discussed it in its relation to love, to the wish to become like the admired person, to make the teacher, his qualities and knowledge, part of oneself.

I have so far talked mainly about conditions of learning and not about learning itself. By doing so I have followed my original plan to choose for my lecture the topic which teachers have asked me most often about, because other approaches to psychology may have given less attention to this aspect. I have done so also in order to stress the nature of the relationship to the teacher, and how it follows on, and differs from, the early relations to the parents.

Present-day education gives the teacher the task of providing opportunities for the child to use. These must be in accordance with the child's capacities as they mature, and must form part of the school curriculum. Seen from this angle, the teacher's role has changed in a similar way as the mother's role has changed regarding meals she provides for the child who has left babyhood.

It has been found that young children thrive when permitted to choose among a variety of dishes. The mother's task from the second year onwards is no longer to decide exactly what the child must have at every meal and to try to force it into him. Her task is now confined to providing a reasonable choice of attractive food, eliminating what is definitely harmful and indigestible, and to leave it to the child's appetite and manual ability to take it in. The modern teacher no longer needs to feel that knowledge has to be 'pushed into' the pupil, either. He learns to count on the child's thirst for knowledge. He is learning, as so many mothers do, that a range of opportunities being provided for him, the child 'takes in' eagerly what he is longing for and that little is gained by providing 'food' that does not attract him. But he needs the teacher's and his parents' approval for a longer time in this achievement.

I have referred to thirst for knowledge, and have made it clear that we rely essentially today on the child's own urge to know, though other factors such as rivalry and need for approval play their part. Freud has many times referred to this and has shown that the child's impetus in his search is derived from his need to discover secrets of a sexual nature, to know about the functions of his own body, the difference between the sexes, the parents' relations, and his own origin. In his study of Leonardo da Vinci (10) he expresses the view that the period of active sexual investigation begins in the third year, and is usually set off by an external event such as the birth of a baby. In this paper Freud discusses the fate curiosity may have, if it remains linked with the sexual aims or becomes detached and sublimated, able to use most of its energy to search for other knowledge.

Its link with the destructive tendencies within the child, and the need to free curiosity from this trend, too, to make it readily available for intellectual use, has grown out of our later knowledge. While on the other hand the effort that is needed for mastery must be supplied by his aggressive instinct.

When the child comes to school the teacher finds the ground prepared; curiosity has undergone its first transformation. This may have been essentially brought about by the parents' response to his early investigations on his own body or the questions put to them. A father who gives the shortest possible answers to any question, the mother who seems ill at ease and says, 'Wait till you are bigger', or the aunt who talks about flowers and bees when the child wants an immediate answer to an urgent question. All three have left him with the feeling that knowledge is not for him, that his inquiries are unwanted, that he incurs a risk in going further. He may, where the risk seems great enough, not dare search further into those directions. Or he may have encountered something in his search which in itself has caused a shock and stopped him on his way. Or the arrest of his activities may have come from *within*, through their link with destructiveness and guilt in his phantasy life.

Where these early attempts have not led to guilt and fear, where the child has found the parents willing and able to follow him and help him in his questions step by step as they arose, a way is open for him to go further, and much of the energy is free for all the other questions that concern the things around him. This freedom to explore is one of the child's features to which the teacher refers later as 'a joy to teach'.

Much depends on the teacher's own attitude to the child's curiosity and on his capacity to share freely what he has. This is an important field in itself for application of psychoanalytic knowledge. As an example: two things teachers have said to me about their work have vividly stayed in my mind because they seemed to me to contain so much of what we try to understand about the differences we find in the results obtained by different teachers, and the conviction that the difference does not lie in their academic knowledge essentially. Once a teacher said to me: 'When I see those fifty-two children look at me and I know that everyone of them wants something from me, it makes me feel quite weak.' And the other, a little middle-aged woman from an isolated school in Australia where she had everybody in one class from five to fourteen, including a defective, said: 'It's hard work, but you see the fun of it is that each of them wants something from me, that each one needs something quite different, and that I know I can supply it.'

The unconscious phantasies at the back of these two feelings are well known to us from work with mothers. For some breastfeeding is a weakening experience; they feel that the child is emptying them out. Others get so much enjoyment from it, not because in fact they have more milk, but because they have built up in their mind a picture of themselves as someone who is strong and able to give others strength, feeling enriched and not impoverished by it.

The role played by defensive measures in the use the child can make of what is supplied to him has been mentioned. Each analysis of children and adults brings further insight into the puzzling problem concerning people who seem normally or even specially endowed and still unable to use these capacities for learning. It is beyond the scope of this paper to deal with the immense variety of unconscious factors which cause restrictions or inhibitions of the use of mental functions. Knowledge of their unconscious nature is in itself a signal for the teacher not to confuse external and internal measures with each other. He can avoid making the child or himself responsible for failure in certain fields; he can avoid putting external pressure on the child, hoping to force him out of a state which is internally controlled. The well-known phrase that goes into thousands of homes every term is frequently the result of such misunderstanding—it reads: 'Could do better if tried harder.'

From all that has been said it is now clear that psychoanalytic understanding has deepened our knowledge of the teacher's role, and that far from being seen as unimportant in the child's development, the special contribution he has to make is given more attention.

In a study carried out by Dr P. Turquet and Miss T. Alcock (11) a way is shown of getting deeper understanding of the teacher's problems by group discussions. The training of teachers and the selection of those who are about to enter the profession can be decisively improved in this direction in the future.

From the co-operation of teachers and analysts who are interested in schools, we can expect great gains for both. This has been found for many years now in the Department of Child Development of the University of London Institute of Education. For the gifted teacher psycho-analysis makes explicit what was implicit in his work before. For others, who cannot rely so safely on their intuition, it brings help through guidance and support.

BIBLIOGRAPHY

(1) HARTMANN, H., and KRIS, E. (1945). 'The Genetic Approach in Psycho-Analysis', *Psycho-Analytic Study of the Child*, Vol. 1.

(2) FREUD, S., *Autobiographical Study*, 2nd ed. London: Hogarth Press, 1946.

(3) ISAACS, S. (1933). *The Social Development in Young Children*. London: Routledge.

(4) FREUD, A., and BURLINGHAM, D. (1942). *Young Children in War-time*. London: Allen & Unwin.

(5) FREUD, A. (1937). *The Ego and the Mechanisms of Defence*. London: Hogarth Press.

(6) *Report of the Committee on Maladjusted Children*. H.M.S.O., 1955.

(7) FREUD, S. (1914). 'Some Reflections on Schoolboy Psychology', *Standard Ed.*, Vol. XIII. London: Hogarth Press, 1955.

(8) FREUD, S. (1918). 'From the History of an Infantile Neurosis', *Collected Papers*, Vol. III. London: Hogarth Press, 1925.

(9) FREUD, A., 'Certain Types and Stages of Social Maladjustment' (in Eissler, K. R., ed: *Searchlights on Delinquency*. London: Imago, 1949).

(10) FREUD, S., *Leonardo da Vinci*. London: Kegan Paul, 1932.

(11) TURQUET, P., and Alcock, T. Unpublished report to Unesco. National Council of Christians and Jews. Some Attitudes in Teachers.

IV

PSYCHO-ANALYSIS AND ART

By Marion Milner, b.sc.

What is art? And what is genius in art? When I set out to prepare this lecture I intended to try to select out of writings on art, both by analysts and non-analysts, whatever might point the direction towards an answer to these questions. I read many books and technical papers on both sides. On the non-analysts' side, for instance, I read Berenson, Kenneth Clarke, William Empson, Gombrich, Susanne Langer, Maritain, André Malraux, and Herbert Read. On the analysts' side I read Freud, Ernest Jones, Ella Sharpe, Anna Freud, Melanie Klein, Balint, Fairbairn, Kris, Hanna Segal, Rycroft, and many others. I also read two who are not analysts but who are identified with the analytic approach—Ehrenzweig and Adrian Stokes. Of course I soon found what an enormous task of digestion I had set myself. Instead of my mind being full of ideas about what art is, it felt a complete blank, so that it seemed quite impossible to achieve any sifting of the various ideas presented by all these writers. Gradually, however, after many weeks, instead of fighting the blankness I became able to accept it. And then I found that certain ideas about what I had read began to emerge of their own accord.

The first one came from the non-analytic side, from Herbert Read's latest book *Icon and Idea* (1), where he says that the great painters, sculptors, poets, and musicians make conquests of consciousness that are afterwards occupied by the mind in widest commonality. He also says that art is finding (rather than seeking) new symbols to signify new areas of sensibility. The next idea came from the analytic side, from Ernst Kris's book *Psychoanalytic Explorations in Art* (2). In this book he tells how, in the sixteenth century for the first time in history, a work of art was considered as a projection of an inner image; for in a contemporary guide-book it was said that a Michelangelo unfinished block was better than the finished one, because it came nearer the state of conception. Hence, says Kris, it is not nearness to reality but nearness to the artist's psychic life that becomes the test of the value of the work of art. Then I found myself haunted by another phrase from the group of non-analytic writers. It was, 'the sovereign awakening of creative subjectivity to itself'. I recognised this as from the French Catholic philosopher Maritain; so I turned to his book *Creative Intuition in Art and Poetry*, (3) where he develops the theme that, as compared with Eastern art, Western art has progressively laid stress on the artist's self. In its last phase, he says, it has plunged deeply into the incommunicable world of creative subjectivity. Here I found my sense of confusion and despairing emptiness had gone, for I felt this phrase 'creative subjectivity' contained a central idea from which to approach the subject of art.

Maritain goes on to talk about the modern painter having become less and less interested in what the painting is of, the something in the outside world that the painting is to be a picture of, and more and more interested in the actual painting. This, he says, has been described as a turning away from nature in favour of an interest in themselves, in their own subjectivity. But, he adds, all this, though true, is only a half-truth. He says that what we see in great modern painting is more interest than ever in nature, but in a different way. He says that the painters are men who, seeking after themselves, are by the same stroke carried along beyond the natural appearance of things in desperate search of a deeper reality. Thus the conquest by brush and palette of this unnameable something is enough for a man to offer up his entire life. And, he says, it is so because creative subjectivity cannot awaken to itself except in communing with things. Thus he maintains, the relation with nature has been changed but has not been abolished.

Now here, in Maritain's description of what the modern

artist is doing, we also get a hint of how he is doing it. For Maritain is saying that it is only through the relation to things that it can happen; by 'things' he means all that is outside the self. Here Freud would have agreed with him. Maritain goes on to try to describe the creative act itself. He says that at the root of the creative act there must be a quite peculiar mental process without parallel in logical reason, a process through which things and the self are grasped together by means of a kind of experience or knowledge which has no conceptual expression and is shown only in the artist's work. He calls this process creative or poetic intuition. And he goes on to say that in poetic intuition, objective reality and subjectivity, the world and the whole of the soul coexist inseparably. He says: 'At that moment sense and sensation are brought back to the heart, blood to the spirit, passion to intuition.' And he adds that this particular intellectual process, which has no parallel in logical reason, is not really a process of liberation from reason because reason possesses a life both deeper and less conscious than its articulate logical life. In poetry, he says, we enter a nocturnal empire, a primeval activity of the intellect which, far beyond concepts and logic, exercises itself in vital connections between imagination and emotion. So here is something else that it does—or a different way of describing the bringing back of blood to the spirit; this time it is bringing together imagination and feeling. Note also that he talks of reason as having a life deeper and less conscious than its articulate* logical life.

Now, this word 'articulate' brought me back again to the analytic side, to a writer who knows about the process of analysis from direct experience, although not himself an analyst; to Ehrenzweig and his book *The Psycho-Analysis of Artistic Vision and Hearing* (4). For here Ehrenzweig talks about what he calls the 'articulating tendency' of the surface mind, and the fact that we tend, for the most part, to notice compact, simple, precise forms, at the same time

* By 'articulate' I think he intends to convey the ordinary dictionary meaning, which is both 'verbalised' and 'organised together'.

eliminating vague, incoherent, inarticulate forms from our perception. He points out how both William James and Freud, independently of each other, drew attention to the articulating tendency of our surface perception. So, he says, did the *Gestalt* psychologists; they used the term '*Gestalt* tendency' to describe how we tend to perceive in terms of compactness and coherence—how we like to see a pattern, find one, even in chaos. Ehrenzweig goes on to tell of how the *Gestalt* psychologists take art as a supreme manifestation of the human mind's striving towards articulate *Gestalt*; but he thinks this theory has led to a failure to appreciate some of the most fundamental aspects of art; that is what he called in a recent broadcast talk 'the role of the creative accident'. He also reminds us that Freud not only noticed the articulating tendency of our observing mind but found that ideas coming from the lower layers of the mind, like our dream visions, tend to be inarticulate; they appear to our observing mind as altogether chaotic and difficult to grasp; and not only our night dreams but also our day dreams have this elusive quality. Of course we do not really need an expert to tell us this. We have only to try to take a look at our own day dreams, reveries, moments of absent-mindedness, to know that we do, ordinarily, think on two different levels, in an oscillating rhythm, and that when we return from the absent-minded phase it is not always easy to say what we have been thinking. In fact, it must be clear to anyone who looks inwards that our mental life does progress with a movement rather like a porpoise. (The old cartoons of the Loch Ness monster perhaps give the best graphic picture of it.)

Ehrenzweig points out how Otto Rank maintained that artistic creativeness involves a cyclical displacement of mental energy between two different levels; yet he considered the inarticulate phase preceding the emergence of ideas as mere interruption of consciousness, emptiness of vision. Here Ehrenzweig refers to William James, and how he said that the creative state wrongly appears as an emptiness of consciousness only because we cannot grasp its fluid content in the definite perceptions of the surface mind. Ehrenzweig concludes that any act of creativeness requires a temporary, cyclical paralysis of the surface attention. He gives an example of such temporary paralysis from an artist sketching in his background forms in a state of diffused attention, a state by which he looks at figure and background in one glance; an impossible task, says Ehrenzweig, from the point of view of *Gestalt* theory. He also talks of the particular technique needed to get hold of the visions filling the creative mind (during the alleged lapse of consciousness), as a kind of absent-minded watchfulness. (This may, by the way, be compared with Freud's description of the kind of attention required of the analyst.) Ehrenzweig also discusses that particular class of people who have foregone the attempt to relate their visions to surface perception—the mystics. He says that when the mystic returns to surface consciousness he has the memory of deeply significant visions but without a trace of definite imagery. Thus the mystic's vision does not appear to him as mere emptiness, and he does not try to project a more elaborate pattern into it, as Freud says we do when we unconsciously give to our night dreams some sort of secondary shape and communicability.

Ehrenzweig goes on to point out how Freud also talked about a mystical state, a state which he described as a feeling of being one with the universe. Freud called it oceanic (a term borrowed from a friend), and he admitted that he had never had it himself. He explained it as a regression to the early infantile state of consciousness, to the state when the child's ego is not yet differentiated from the surrounding external world. Hence, says Ehrenzweig, Freud is claiming that the feeling of union is no mere illusion, but the correct description of a memory of an infantile state otherwise inaccessible to direct introspection. Ehrenzweig adds a further explanation, one based on Freud's own discoveries about the form of thinking in dreams. He says that the mystic feeling is explained by our rational surface mind's incapacity to visualise the inarticulate images of the depth mind, and his central point is that the creative process takes place in these gaps in our surface mind's activity. He goes on to point out how these rhythms of the mind can be seen as a series; it ranges from the rapid oscillations of everyday thinking and perception to the slower cycle of waking and sleeping and to the even slower double rhythm of the creative activity in which the submerged phase may be sometimes extremely protracted.

What Ehrenzweig does, I think, imply but not state is what Maritain states so clearly; that is, that this process which goes on in the gaps essentially involves an undoing of that split into subject and object which is the very basis of our logical thinking. Ehrenzweig says that it also follows that the depth mind can do things that the surface mind cannot do. It can encompass a complexity of relationships that is quite beyond the capacity of the surface mind. He talks of this as the unconscious sense of form, and says it can only be reached by the diffused, wide stare, not by the narrow focus of ordinary attention. He maintains that it is this wide focus which makes it possible for the artist to get closer to a more primitive vision of the world, a vision which can appear confused and chaotic to the adult mind but is not really so; it is not chaotic, only more generalised. He also offers evidence that the perception of time relations in the depth mind is different from that of the surface mind. He says that the depth mind is not, for instance, limited by the surface mind's preference for time relations which only go one way; in fact, it can perceive time relations backwards just as easily as forwards.

These ideas of Ehrenzweig interested me very much, especially the emphasis on the wide diffused stare of attention. For when I first began, thirty years ago, to try to observe from inside—that is, introspectively—the effect of different ways of looking at the outside world, I discovered that it was just this wide focus of attention that made the world seem most intensely real and significant.

The state of mind which analysts describe as a repetition of the infant's feelings in its mother's arms, the state

which Freud called oceanic, is thus being regarded by
certain writers on art as an essential part of the creative
process. But it is not the oceanic feeling by itself, for that
would be the mystic's state; it is rather the oceanic state in a
cyclic oscillation with the activity of what Ehrenzweig calls
the surface mind, with that activity in which 'things' and the
self, as Maritain puts it, are grasped separately, not together.
And the cyclic oscillation is not just passively experienced
but actively used, with the intent to make something,
produce something.

FIG. 1.

Fig. 1 shows a doodle drawing made by a patient in
analysis. She had had some experiences near to those that
mystics talk about, though she had not called it mystical.
This drawing will give you the opportunity of observing in
yourselves a moment of oscillating perception; when you
look steadily at it you will see that it alternates between
being a single face seen from the front, with a lock of hair
down the middle, and two faces looking at each other, seen
in profile. Fig. 2 shows another of this patient's drawings;
the top face is uncertain about its boundary and the lower
part of the drawing oscillates between being one full face,
round like the sun, and two profiles. Fig. 3 is a tracing of the

lower half so that it can be seen more clearly. My interpretation of this drawing is that the full face does represent
the state of feeling of oneness with the universe, the un-
divided state, while the profiles represent the phase of separation, of twoness, of differentiation of oneself from others.

Now I will turn to another writer, also a non-analyst, but
deeply identified with the psycho-analytic approach, one
who has written many highly interesting studies of works of
art—Adrian Stokes (5). I will quote what he says, not about
the state of mind in which a work of art is produced, but
about the work of art itself. Stokes talks of a work of art as
an individual separate object, differentiated yet made
of undifferentiated material, something that suggests an
entirely separate entity yet having a pulse in common and
joined to the heart of things. He says that this is what the
artist strives to recreate, a sense of fusion, thus renewing the
oceanic feeling but combined with object 'otherness'. And
he says that it is from this state of fusion in which ideas are
interchangeable that the poetic identifications flow.

At this point, instead of seeking further amongst the
writings of analysts or non-analysts, I am going to do what
Freud himself, in 1932 (6), advised one to do, when science
seemed not yet able to provide an answer to a problem. He
said, 'ask the poets'; but the subject he was searching for
light upon at that moment was not art but femininity. So I
am going to remind you of a work of art which combines
the vision of two poets; the one ancient Hebrew, the other
late eighteenth- and early nineteenth-century English. It
is Blake's *Illustrations to the Book of Job*.

This work of Blake's (I am talking of the final version,
published in 1826) consists of twenty-one engravings with
texts from the Bible and linear drawings set around the
margins. You remember the story of Job, the perfect and
upright man; how Satan appears before God and says it's
all very well for Job to be so good when he has everything
he could possibly want, but what if he really suffered, would
he be so good then? So God gives Satan permission to plague
Job in every possible way short of killing him. Fig. 4, for

Figs. 2 and 3
Oscillating
perspective.
Doodle drawing

Fig. 5 Job with his wife and family

Fig. 4 Satan smiting Job's sons and daughters

Fig. 7 Job with his daughters

Fig. 6 Job with his family restored

Fig. 9 Arrival of Elihu

Fig. 8 God appears, as a demon

Fig. 10 Satan leaps in before the Throne

Fig. 11 Satan smiting Job with boils

Fig. 13 The God of Eliphaz

Fig. 12 The Morning Stars sang together

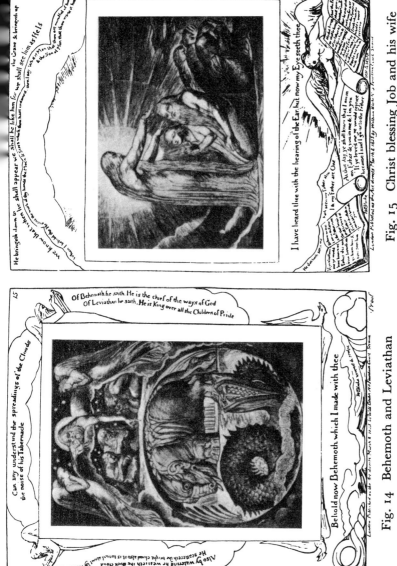

Fig. 15   Christ blessing Job and his wife

Fig. 14   Behemoth and Leviathan

Fig. 16   Copy of Christ picture

Fig. 17   Copy of Eliphaz picture

instance, shows Satan killing Job's sons and daughters. And you remember how Job at first bears all patiently, but finally succumbs and curses the day he was born. And then when Job has reached the depths of despair a new figure appears, Elihu; and after this Job gradually climbs back to his original estate—but with a difference. Now Blake has made it quite clear that he is using this ancient story in a special way in order to say something about the stultification of creative expression in the arts. In the first picture (Fig. 5) of Job with his wife and family, surrounded by his flocks, they are all shown grouped under a spreading tree upon which hang musical instruments, unused. Job is reading from a book and one of the texts says, 'The letter killeth, the spirit giveth life'. The last picture (Fig. 6), showing Job with his family and flocks restored to him, has the same design, but now they are all singing or playing upon their instruments. And the picture immediately before the last (Fig. 7) is of Job in his own house with paintings upon the walls, and grouped around him are his three daughters. The texts say: 'There were not found women as fair as the daughters of Job in all the land and their father gave them inheritance among their brethren.' Blake also makes it quite clear what the three daughters signify, because in another picture (not included in the Job series) Job is shown surrounded by the three allegorical figures of painting, poetry, and music.

The first eleven pictures of Blake's version show the gradual stages of Job's downfall and descent to the depths—from the second picture, where Satan appears before the throne of God (and God has the same face as Job), up to the climax (Fig. 8), where the God Job has called upon appears, but as a demon (though still with the face of Job himself). Then come the stages of the recovery, beginning with the advent of Elihu (Fig. 9).

If one asks: What is Blake's view about why Job had to go through such torment, the answer is clear. There is no doubt from Blake's choice of texts throughout the series that, for him, the nature of Job's error was two-fold. In the first place his mistake was that he thought he was perfect because his conscious intention was perfect; Job lived, as he thought, in perfect obedience to his God according to the letter of the law. And he could do this because he thought that what he was conscious of in himself was all there was; so he is shown persistently denying that there could be any evil in himself just because his conscious intention is not evil. But Blake is quite clear that in Job's inner world there is evil; 'that which is above is within', says Blake elsewhere. So in the second picture (Fig. 10) Job's inner world is shown above his head and in it is Satan, the principle of destruction, leaping in and demanding expression.

In the second place, Blake seems to be saying that there is a mistake in Job's whole attitude of mind in respect of what Blake seems to call maleness and femaleness; for he clearly shows that he thinks Job's attitude is one-sidedly male. Thus Job is shown not only as obeying the letter of the law and thinking that is all there is, he is also shown as a successful patriarch, a man of power; and the idea that he is leaving something out of count, to which Blake gives the name of female, is expressed in various ways. For instance (Fig. 11), when Satan stands astride him, smiting him with boils, Job is shown repudiating his wife, who kneels weeping at his feet. If we are interested in the dark side of consciousness as containing, amongst other things, all those wishes that we have repudiated because they are incompatible with our standards and idea of ourselves, then we could certainly find plenty to say here about the conflicts in a man as a man (Job here standing for all men) about women as women. But if we are also interested in the nature of the processes in the dark side of consciousness, as I am here, then I think it is clear that the figure of Job's wife does also stand for an unadmitted way of functioning in himself. I think this is a legitimate interpretation in the light of the ideas expressed in the pictures of the recovery. For not only is there the picture of the restoring of Job's daughters before his sons, there is also in the famous 'Morning Stars' picture (Fig. 12; the third after the appearance of Elihu), the moon goddess (driving a team of serpents) given equal prominence with the sun god driving a team of horses. Also there is an interesting recurrent theme of the position of the arms in the pictures of the recovery, both those of the Deity and of Job. They gradually become spread out in a wide, embracing gesture; and this is surely significant in connection with that wide-focused, wide-embracing kind of attention which Ehrenzweig claims is characteristic of the functioning of what he calls the depth mind. By contrast (Fig. 13), there is Blake's picture of the God of Job's friend Eliphaz, as seen by Job in a dream; you will notice the arms are tightly bound, not wide-embracing.

Most interesting of all, perhaps, to the psycho-analyst if not to the artist, is the picture after the 'Morning Stars' (the fourth after the arrival of Elihu, Fig. 14). In it the Deity is shown lying on a cloud, and drawing the attention of Job and his wife and friends to what is obviously an inner world—because enclosed in a circle—but this time down below. In it are the two monsters, Behemoth and Leviathan. What did Blake mean by this picture? Like all poetic symbolism, it must have manifold meaning. But as I see it and in the setting of the problem of creativeness, we are back on the theme of the two levels of the mind—the surface or conscious mind and the depth or unconscious mind. For Behemoth seems to be standing on the land, though looking rather angry about it; and Leviathan is certainly half submerged in water, and looks as if about to go under, though whether in a swoon of agony or ecstasy it is hard to say. The fact that Blake shows the Leviathan figure, the figure related to the depths, as half serpent, suggests that he does think of Leviathan as related to, if not identical with, a primitive form of the female aspect of the psyche; for it is the moon goddess who drives serpents. However, as against my theory, I must admit that Blake calls Leviathan 'he', and puts the text: 'Of Leviathan he said, he is King over all the children of pride'; but perhaps this is not as contradictory to my argument as appears at first sight. Certainly in this picture Blake seems to be showing his idea of the basic human energies in their most primitive form, for both creatures have a look of blind, unseeing eyes, as if to express the idea of energy not yet aware of itself. Thus it seems to me that Blake is developing in these pictures, following the arrival of Elihu, an idea of the same kind of happening in human development as that described by Maritain when he talks of 'the awakening of creative subjectivity to itself'. Also Blake seems to be saying that this awakening comes through the acceptance of, equally with the male, what he seems to look upon as the female phase of mental functioning; also that the full experience of this female phase means a willingness to accept a temporary submergence below the surface consciousness.

Blake also implies, I think, that this phase or state that he calls female is not concerned primarily with the boundaries that mark off the self from the rest of the world. For in the marginal drawings of the Elihu picture the spirits which emanate from Job's sleeping body reach out to the stars; as if Blake wished to indicate that a process is here going on which undoes the over-fixed separation between self and other, self and the universe. Thus it seems that having once achieved the sense of separate existence, it is then necessary to be continually undoing it again, in a cyclic oscillation, if psychic sterility is to be avoided.

This idea of undoing a separation is also developed in the seventeenth picture of the series (Fig. 15). Here Christ appears standing on the ground beside Job and his wife, and blessing them, while the friends shrink away in terror. Several of the texts here are from the Gospels. One of them says: 'I and my Father are one'; also 'And that day ye shall know that I am in my Father and you in me and I in you'.

If one asks the question, why does Blake bring the figure of Christ into the Job story? I think the answer is quite clear. He does it because he really does feel that the teachings of Christ have something to do with creative process, whether in art or science. For instance, in his poem 'Jerusalem' he says: 'I know of no other Christianity and of no other

Gospel than the liberty both of mind and body to exercise
the Divine Arts of Imagination. . . . The Apostles knew of no
other Gospel . . . O ye Religious, discountenance every one
among you who shall pretend to despise Art and Science.'

Also in the same poem he says:

'O Human Imagination! O Divine Body I have crucified!'

Thus he certainly does seem to be saying that this state
of oneness has something to do with creative process, both
in science and art; and also that the working of this creative
power requires an active surrender of the purposive,
controlling, deliberative mind. 'That he may withdraw
Man from his purpose and hide Pride from Man', says one
of the texts to the Elihu picture. You will notice that I said
'active surrender', for it is not a blind surrender; as André
Malraux says in his book, *The Voices of Silence* (7), art is
certainly not a complete capitulation to the unconscious.
Thus in the light of these pictures I think there is no doubt
what Blake thought about the flowering of creative process.
He is saying it depends on giving equal validity to a state
of mind which is attentive and receptive to what is happening (symbolised by the female), equally with the state that
tries to force what happens into a preconceived idea or
pattern. But let no one suppose that because it is that it is
therefore easy; it is an ordeal, what Maritain calls the 'inner
ordeal of creative freedom', when discussing Chardin's
words, 'He who has not felt the difficulties of his art does
nothing that counts'. And there is discipline involved,
though not the kind that is imposed from above by practice
in following rules. It is rather a struggling to let something
happen in relation to a chosen material, that malleable
bit of the external world which can be shaped. And it is by
this struggle with the material that the conscious mind
disciplines the chaotic forces in the creative depths.

Some such conception of the nature of the creative process
is also necessary, I think, for the full understanding of
Freud's work and discoveries. For what he invented was, in
fact, an instrument for the study of the psyche—and one that
at the same time was an instrument of healing. For his

patients the medium to be manipulated was a vocal sound, the action required of them was simply that they should talk —or, as a present-day analyst, Clifford Scott, has put it, make a noise—without trying to impose any standards of logic, order, politeness, or decency. And by this free talking, or free association as Freud called it, his patients began to discover what it was they really thought. They did it by gradually becoming able to hear what they said (like E. M. Forster's old lady who said, 'How can I know what I think till I see what I say'). Freud discovered that his role was simply to listen and try to help them see the implications of what they had said. And the result was, when things went well, that the patients began to be able to relate themselves more fully, both to the hidden creative roots of their existence, and to what is offered in the real world, and so became able to free their powers of loving and working. In fact, I think it could be said, although Freud himself did not say it in just this way, that what he found was this: that the people who came to him were in trouble over a failure to discover how to manage their own feelings and desires, because they were trying to manage them by means of a one-sided kind of thinking which did not, in fact, work. They had been trying to solve problems of feeling by means of the kind of thinking which divides what we see from ourselves seeing it, the kind of thinking which we call logical and for which we have formulated laws—the primary laws of logic; such as, for instance, that a thing is what it is and is not what it is not; or that something cannot both be and not be at the same time. He found also that these people were intensely preoccupied and influenced in their feelings and behaviour, in an irrational way, by a different kind of thinking, a kind which did not work according to the laws of logic, a kind which Freud called unconscious phantasy. Thus it seemed as if they were trying to live their lives as though conscious, common-sense, logical thinking was all there was—for good or for ill—just as Job had done, and it was only when they found that they could not solve their problems by reasoning with themselves that Freud was called in to help. And it was then that he found, by attending to what they freely imagined rather than to their common-sense reasoning, that they were helped to a freeing of their powers.

But this other way of thinking (which Freud and psychoanalysts after him call phantasy), which is not based on making that rigid distinction between subjective and objective that logical thinking does, has some relation to what Maritain describes as the poetic activity. He talks of a margin of dreaming activity which many have murdered within themselves, by which the soul is known in the experience of the world and the world is known in the experience of the soul. He says that it is a knowledge which does not know itself, for such knowledge knows not in order to know but in order to produce. His central claim is that, apart from the process which tends to knowledge by means of concepts, there is also something which is preconceptual, not a mere way to the concept but another kind of germ which does not tend towards a concept to be formed. Such a thing is knowledge in act, a kind of inherent knowledge which, he says, is of the essence of poetry. But it is not only Maritain who talks about this inherent kind of knowing; descriptions of it can be found in poetry itself. For instance, Thomas Traherne in the seventeenth century wrote:

> It acts not from its centre to
> Its object as remote,
> But present is, when it doth view,
> Being with the Being it doth note.
> Whatever it doth do,
> It doth not by another engine work,
> But by itself; which in the act doth lurk.

Maritain also talks about the substance of man being obscure to himself; he knows not his own subjectivity, or if he does, only as a kind of propitious or enveloping night; he says subjectivity as such cannot be conceptualised, it is an unknowable abyss—which is perhaps what the Chinese say more concisely when they say:

'The Tao of which we speak is not the real Tao.'

I hope these last quotations will give you some idea of the difficulty of talking logically about this other half of thinking, which Blake calls female and which he insists must be given 'equal inheritance' if there is not to be psychic sterility.

Now I want to go back to Job's other mistake, his denial of his own destructiveness. For this much is clear, to a Freudian at least: Job's perfect obedience left out of count all his rebellion and anger at not being himself as omnipotent as he once, as an infant, thought he was. Classical Freudian theory would say that, by perfect obedience, Job has tried to regain that lost omnipotence, tried to regain it by being one with God. A Freudian would say also that the state described in the text to the second picture (Fig. 13), 'When the Almighty was yet with me, when my children were about me', is a description of the original oceanic feeling of infancy when one had, as Freud said, 'the notion of limitless extension and oneness with the universe'. Thus Job's anger, as shown in the person of Satan, can be seen as his infantile destructive anger at being forced by the impacts of external reality to give up that feeling.

With this theme of destructiveness I want to go back to the subject of symbols and to Herbert Read's remark about art as the finding of symbols. For it is a fact that more and more analysts are now becoming concerned with the way in which symbols are created; and this includes, of course, the problem of the creation of concepts, for verbal concepts are only a special class of symbols. Analysts find that in their most deeply disturbed patients the process of symbol formation has been interfered with, or perhaps never properly established. And two ideas are emerging from this. First, that the achieving of a symbol (a symbol being seen as essentially a substitute) involves a mourning for the loss of that for which it is a substitute. Second, that the process of finding the substitute requires a temporary merging of the idea of the original thing with the idea of the substitute. Now, this idea of the experience of loss as an essential aspect of symbol formation does, I think, provide a bridge between Maritain's formulation and the psycho-analyst's. For

Maritain, in talking about Dante, speaks of 'Some abiding despair in every great poet, a certain wound in him that has set free the creativeness'. What psycho-analysis is adding is that where there is such a wound or loss, then there is also, implicit or explicit, anger at the loss. There is certainly plenty of anger in Dante, expressed in the tortures he gives to the souls of the damned; also in Blake's pictures, such as the one of Satan destroying Job's sons and daughters.

At this stage in my argument I think the names that have been given to the two phases of the mind's oscillation become important. For instance, Ehrenzweig borrows from Nietzsche the terms Apollonian and Dionysian. He says that Greek tragedy grew from the Dionysian mysteries, expressive of fear, anguish, cravings for self-destruction and mystic union with the universe. It is most interesting that he makes this link between self-destruction and mystic union (as religions have so often done) because it has a bearing on what Freud called the death instinct or Thanatos, which he postulated as the inescapable pair of the life instinct or Eros. Freudians, at least some of them, say that the so-called death instinct aims at self-destruction; but they do not, as a rule, go on to say that this self-destruction is perhaps a distorted, because frustrated, form of that self-surrender which is inherent in creative process. But Ehrenzweig says so, and I think that Blake implies it. Ehrenzweig thinks that Dionysian Thanatos is the chaotic life force which tries to break up individual existence, while Apollonian Eros is the form principle of differentiation which safeguards individual existence by moulding the Dionysian chaos into order and beauty. Incidentally, I should like to mention that Ehrenzweig follows up this idea about the ordering of the Dionysian chaos with a discussion on the nature of 'beauty' and 'style'. It is a discussion which is made rather confusing, though full of interesting observations, because he does not make it sufficiently clear that he is limiting the concepts of beauty and style to what can be talked about and analysed by the aesthetician. I think he has artificially restricted the meaning of these concepts in order to get round the undoubted difficulty that what he is talking about is something which cannot, in fact, be analysed without destroying it, but can only be appreciated. And this, I feel, is also my chief difficulty in this lecture; I am trying to talk about a state of mind that does in a sense stop being that state of mind as soon as we separate ourselves from it sufficiently to talk about it in logical terms.

This theme of Thanatos brings us to the theory of artistic creation developed by Melanie Klein and her followers, particularly Hanna Segal (8). Ehrenzweig takes account of this work and describes it as conceiving the creative process as a primary, psychic disintegration, both of the self and of the image of what is loved in the external world, under the direct influence of the Thanatos urges, together with an acceptance of this double destruction, an acceptance which allows the artist to rebuild both the destroyed self and the destroyed loved object in the aesthetic experience of art. This approach has been vividly illustrated in Adrian Stokes's recent book on Michelangelo. He describes how Michelangelo suffered acutely from anxiety and depression, and the central theme of the book is built round Michelangelo's own phrase 'That he lived on anxiety and death'. Stokes maintains that an artist of this type can do this because he can transmute anxiety and death into the sublime forms of his art. The book aims to show, says Herbert Read in his review of it, that the very greatness of Michelangelo's art is due to a superhuman effort to repair this tormented psyche. Of course, some critics will say that not all great artists had such tormented psyches, and that it is unwise to generalise about the nature of art from such an extreme case. If we turn to Blake again for light on this problem, he certainly has plenty to say about psychic torment as part of the state of psychic sterility if not as an inherent part of psychic creativity; as, for instance, in the picture of the climax of Job's descent when the God he has called upon appears as the devil, and his friends have become demons pulling him down into the fires of the pit.

Now, as I have said, the theme of denial of destructiveness, denial of Thanatos, seems to be one theme in Blake's Job, but only one, the other being to do with the repudiation of that state of mind which Blake calls female and which has something to do with a submergence of consciousness. Now, the difference between these two themes could perhaps be restated in terms of the difference between the content of unconscious thought processes and the form of them. Thus the content of our unconscious thoughts includes, according to Freud's discoveries, the history of the battle between our loving and our hating from earliest infancy. But, and this is what Ehrenzweig is saying, it is also the form of our unconscious thinking that must be considered in any attempt to find out what art is. Thus I think it is true to say that any attempt to explain art solely in terms of the history of wishes (that is, in terms of the genesis of adult powers of loving from their earlier forms in infantile loving) seems to artists themselves, and to the sensitive art critic, to be leaving something out.

Here I wish to go back to Maritain who, in the same book from which I have already quoted, makes a direct attack on Freud. He says that the disregard of the poetic function by psycho-analysis is both a sign of the dullness of our times and is why the explanations of psycho-analysts have proved particularly unfortunate in the domain of art—and, he adds, of religion. How can this criticism be answered? Or can it be answered at all? Perhaps what I have deduced from Blake's Job, and also what Ehrenzweig says about the relation of the surface mind to the depth mind, can point a direction from which an answer could come. For in these terms it looks as if Maritain is saying that any 'explanation' of art which is only in terms of the content of repressed wishes, what Gombrich calls the artist's complexes, leaves out what is essential and perhaps specific to art. It leaves out this deliberately fostered getting in touch with, not just hidden wishes but a different way of functioning; and a way of functioning which is essential if something new is to be created. This is why I think Gombrich (9) said (in his Ernest Jones Lecture) that many people feel the attempt to

deduce an artist's complexes from his work to be irrelevant.
And it is for this reason that I am not here going to discuss
such famous writings as, for instance, Freud on Leonardo
da Vinci nor Ella Sharpe on King Lear, nor even Ernest
Jones on Hamlet. For in all these the emphasis is on the
content of the wishes revealed, not on the specific processes
which make it possible for the creative artist to embody the
wishes in such meaningful symbols. But there are writings
of analysts who do attempt to describe the nature of the
specific process in the artist. Here I will mention again
Kris's book, because this, although entirely psycho-analytic
in approach, does provide a bridge in the direction of
Maritain's conceptions. For Kris does come to a conclusion
about the specific capacity of the artist. Like Ehrenzweig, he
says it is to do with a special kind of interplay between
two levels of functioning; but he puts this conclusion in
technical terms and talks about 'a controlled regression of
the ego to the primary process'. This is not the place to go
into the meaning of the term 'primary process'; I only
mention it in order to show that Kris does see the creative
process as a deliberate reversion to a different, more child-
like way of functioning. Incidentally, I think there are signs
that a revision of the concept 'primary process' is already in
the air, a revision that has been partly stimulated by the
problems raised by the nature of art.

In my own attempts to study the nature of creative processes, I have become more and more aware of the anxiety
which accompanies such deliberate reversion to a more
primitive process. Ehrenzweig also emphasises this as an
essential part of creation, not only because of getting nearer
to forbidden wishes, but just because the depth mind's way
of working seems like chaos to the surface mind. Stokes also
hints that it is the seemingly chaotic form of the depth mind,
as well as fear of the destructive wishes, that contribute to
the creative agonies of the artist; for he says: 'Art, if only
by implication, bears witness to the world of depression and
chaos overcome.' About twelve years ago, when first
beginning to study these pictures of Blake's, I felt a rather

blind urge to get past the richness of the ideas and poetic thought portrayed in them, and to see more clearly the purely graphic formal qualities of feeling. So I made a rough copy of the Christ picture, using only the pattern of darks and lights and leaving out all the linear detail (Fig. 16). In spite of doing this, it was years before I could bring myself to face the, to me, intensely disturbing quality of the masses on the right, which seem to be breaking away from the circular forms surrounding the figure of Christ. In fact, not until writing this lecture did I really become able to face the full significance of the terror of the Christ figure shown by Job's friends. Now I can link it with the fears roused in the logical argumentative mind by the impact of the creative depths, and see that the anxiety is not something to be retreated from, but that it is inherent in the creative process itself. I also made a similar copy of the picture of Job's dream of the God of Eliphaz (Fig. 17). Here the most striking thing to me, in the purely feeling aspect of the picture, was the great, dark, empty space above Job's dreaming head—a pregnant emptiness. And this idea of a pregnant emptiness leads on to another observation. It is that if this feeling of emptiness, of something 'without form and void', can be deliberately accepted, not denied, then the sequel can be an intense richness and fullness of perception, a sense of the world newborn, a feeling which I think is what Blake has sought to express in his picture 'When the Morning Stars sang together' (Fig. 12).

To go back to Maritain's criticism; I think the most relevant answer is given by Ehrenzweig (by implication). He talks of how Freud did, in fact, discover the inarticulate structure of the depth mind through his work on dreams; but he became so busy with the startling therapeutic results of translating the dreams' inarticulate thought into rational language that he did, in fact, neglect the importance of this very inarticulate structure of the unconscious processes which he had himself discovered. Ehrenzweig suggests that this neglect mattered little in clinical work, but it did matter when it came to aesthetics. In other words, Freud became so interested in the content of unconscious phantasies that he neglected their structural form, even though it was he who had first enunciated the laws of that form. Susanne Langer is one of the non-analytic writers who recognises his achievement here. She points out that the first systematic study of what she calls the 'canons of symbolisation' or 'the laws of non-discursive expressive form', as compared with the laws of logical or discursive form, was undertaken by Freud, and that their main logically disturbing features were named by him the principles of overdetermination, condensation, and ambivalence.

Maritain also grumbles at psycho-analysis for being concerned exclusively, he says, with what he calls the animal unconscious. I think there is a clear answer here. It was Rickman who said, in a public lecture in 1936, that man is a phantasying animal. Also Susanne Langer (10) has maintained that what differentiates man from animals is the capacity to make and use symbols. Obviously we do share with animals, and have brought with us from our animal inheritance, a vital interest in sex and sex organs; the race would not continue if we had not. And equally obviously, our sexual urges do come into conflict with the needs of society, as do also our aggressive urges. But, and this is the point, out of this conflict we have developed another capacity—that for symbol formation. Originally, so the biologists tell us, the titanic forces of the life force which at first only reproduced itself by the method of splitting did invent another way; it discovered that the bringing together of two creatures with different functions brought more variety in the offspring. Perhaps it would not be too far-fetched to say that the second greatest invention of nature's after sexual reproduction, was the invention of the psychic process by which, not two different organisms but two different ideas can come together and produce a new idea which yet contains some elements of both the original ideas; in fact, the invention of the power to make symbols.

Herbert Read (11) said, in his Ernest Jones Lecture, that psycho-analysis had done incalculable service to art by showing that art is symbolisation from the beginning, and that the process of symbolic transformation, which is fundamental to the creative process in art, is also biologically fundamental, thus proving that the artist's feeling that what he was doing was not just escapism was right. It follows from this that what is most important about this thing we call a work of art, that is admittedly a symbol, is not the original primary unconscious wish or wishes that it symbolises but the fact that a new thing has been created. A new bit of the outside world, which is not the original primary object of the wish, has been made interesting and significant. Thus the original tremendous primary drive to physical union with another living being has been able to transform itself into interest in every conceivable and inconceivable thing in the universe—by means of the process of symbolisation.

I will try to summarise. The central idea of my paper is that the unconscious mind, by the very fact of its not clinging to the distinction between self and other, seer and seen, can do things that the conscious logical mind cannot do. By being more sensitive to the samenesses rather than the differences between things, by being passionately concerned with finding 'the familiar in the unfamiliar' (which, by the way, Wordsworth says is the whole of the poet's business), it does just what Maritain says it does; it brings back blood to the spirit, passion to intuition. It provides the source for all renewal and re-birth, when old symbols have gone stale. It is, in fact, what Blake calls each man's poetic genius.

I have come to the conclusion that the discovery of the nature of this capacity, a discovery which can be described as the awakening of creative subjectivity to itself, is illustrated by Blake in the Job series beginning with the appearance of Elihu; also that Blake means to show that it is a very new development, as compared with the millions of years of blind living, when he puts in the margin of the Elihu picture the text: 'I am young and ye are very old wherefore I was afraid.' And I think Blake is also implying the same idea when he brings the figure of Christ into his study of creative sterility. In fact, I think he implies, although he does not actually say so, that he believes that it is the creative contact with the unsplit 'depth' mind that Christ was talking about, in poetic terms, in such phrases as 'Take no thought for the morrow . . .', and 'Consider the lilies of the field, they toil not neither do they spin . . .'. So I would hazard a very rough guess as to the way in which it may be possible to formulate an answer to the question 'What is art?' a guess that has grown out of my own experience of using the method Freud invented for observing unconscious processes. Can we say that it is to do with the capacity of the conscious mind to have the experience of co-operating with the unconscious depths, by means of the battle to express something with the chosen medium? If so, then perhaps it is true to say that the measure of genius in the arts is linked up with the extent to which the artist does succeed in co-operating with his unconscious mind by means of his medium.

BIBLIOGRAPHY

(1) READ, Herbert (1955). *Icon and Idea*. London: Faber & Faber.
(2) KRIS, E. (1953). *Psychoanalytic Explorations in Art*. London: Allen & Unwin.
(3) MARITAIN, J. (1953). *Creative Intuition in Art and Poetry*. New York: McClelland.
(4) EHRENZWEIG, A. *The Psycho-Analysis of Artistic Vision and Hearing*. London: Routledge & Kegan Paul, 1953; 'The Mastery of Creative Anxiety', *Art and Artists*. Berkeley: University of California, 1956; 'The Modern Artist and the Creative Accident', *The Listener*, January 12th, 1956.
(5) STOKES, A., 'Form in Art', *New Directions in Psycho-Analysis*, ed. Melanie Klein. London: Tavistock Publications, 1955; *Michelangelo: A Study in the Nature of Art*. London: Tavistock Publications, 1955.
(6) FREUD, S., *Introductory Lectures on Psycho-Analysis: Civilisation and its Discontents*. London: Hogarth Press, 1949.

(7) MALRAUX, A. (1954). *The Voices of Silence*. London: Secker and Warburg.

(8) SEGAL, H., 'The Psycho-analytic Approach to Aesthetics', *New Directions in Psycho-Analysis*, ed. Melanie Klein. London: Tavistock Publications, 1955.

(9) GOMBRICH, E. H. (Ernest Jones Lecture), 'Psycho-analysis and the History of Art', *Int. J. of Psycho-Anal.*, Vol. XXXV, 1954.

(10) LANGER, S., *Feeling and Form*. London: Routledge & Kegan Paul, 1953; *Philosophy in a New Key*. Harvard University Press, 1942.

(11) READ, HERBERT (Ernest Jones Lecture), 'Psycho-analysis and the Problem of Aesthetic Value', *Int. J. of Psycho-Anal.*, Vol. XXXII, 1951.

See also:

MILNER, MARION (Joanna Field), *A Life of One's Own*. London: Chatto & Windus, 1934; *An Experiment in Leisure*. London: Chatto & Windus, 1937; *On Not Being Able to Paint*. London: Heinemann, 1950, and New York: International Universities Press.

V

PSYCHO-ANALYSIS AND PHILOSOPHY

By R. MONEY-KYRLE, M.A., PH.D.

MOST sciences have their roots in philosophy, and academic psychology is no exception to this rule. It was, in fact, the last to break away and become an independent discipline. But psycho-analysis—that new science created by Freud—sprang from medicine rather than from academic psychology. Probably for this reason, philosophers and psychoanalysts have so far taken little interest in each other's work. And what interest there was at the beginning tended to be more hostile than co-operative. Of course there were always exceptions; but, on the whole, philosophers, so far as they took notice of psycho-analysis at all, condemned its basic concepts as muddled and self-contradictory. And analysts silently responded by dismissing philosophy, or at least classical philosophy, as a symptom of obsessional neurosis.

I think both criticisms exaggerate an element of truth which each side has gradually become more able to admit. If so, perhaps the time is ripe for more co-operation. I believe philosophy can be useful to the analyst—particularly in his attempts to reconstruct the development of the child's picture of the world. And a psycho-analytic approach to some problems of classical philosophy could be of interest to the philosopher. So I should like to say something—if only tentatively—about both, beginning with the second.

A Paradox in the Definition of Philosophy

As my point of departure, I will take a question which has the deceptive appearance of being simple: What is philosophy as distinct from other disciplines? A good historical definition, from Russell's *History of Western Philosophy* (1946), is that philosophy lies between science and religion. Scientific questions demand empirical answers, and scientific statements are designed to be tested by observation. The answers to religious questions, on the other hand, though supported by empirical arguments, are primarily based on faith and revelation. The problems of classical philosophy would seem to differ from both of these. They were not expected to be solved by observation; or, if they were, they ceased to be philosophical. Nor were they to be solved by acts of faith, but by reason.

Now, philosophy is much concerned with paradoxes, so that we need not be surprised to find one already in its definition. But this first paradox is certainly startling. For while most classical philosophers would probably have agreed that philosophy consists in the pursuit of synthetic knowledge by pure reason, the logical positivists claim to have proved that there can be no such thing. In other words, according to some of the most distinguished of modern philosophers, there can be no such thing as philosophy in the classical sense. This was the view of my own teacher, Moritz Schlick. It was still more uncompromisingly expressed by Witgenstein (1), in whose opinion a teacher of philosophy should leave philosophical propositions to the learner, and content himself with pointing out that they were meaningless. Of course, this should not be taken to imply that classical philosophers accomplished nothing. They contributed enormously to logic and mathematics on the one hand, and to all the sciences, especially psychology, on the other. But in the narrow sense in which we have been trying to define it, this would seem not to be philosophy.

We can evade the paradox by redefining philosophy as a kind of advance-guard to science engaged in constructing, criticising, and clarifying our overall pictures, or models, of the world—for this is what most philosophers have actually done. But such a definition would not have satisfied those whose aim it was to prove *a priori*, and without reference to experience, that their models were necessarily true. It is precisely this which has been the aim of so much classical philosophy. And it is precisely this which, according to the critics, is not only an impracticable but an illogical demand.

I have stressed the point because it inevitably raises a problem of interest to psychology: Whence came this craving for synthetic *a priori* knowledge; that is, for something logically impossible?*

Motives for Philosophy

Most professions have motives peculiar to themselves, and we may suppose that philosophy is no exception to the rule. Curiosity, one would think, must play a major role. But so it does in science—and also in other matters which philosopher and scientist alike would regard as merely trivial. We have therefore to inquire whether there is anything specific about philosophical curiosity.

The first point to notice about curiosity in general is that it often gets inhibited. Even the proverbial curiosity of children is already diverted from its original aim—not so much because it is rebuffed, as because it is unconsciously derived from a kind of aggressive intrusiveness, akin to greed, for which they unconsciously expect retaliation from their parents (2).

That curiosity is unconsciously felt as dangerous seems strange to modern man, but the ancients took this for granted. They consciously believed it impious to know more than the gods had chosen to reveal. For this impiety, for eating the fruit of the Tree of Knowledge, Adam and all his descendants are said to have deserved eternal punishment. Perhaps the fear of it was greater among the people of the Old Testament than among others. At any rate, they concentrated on religion, and avoided both philosophy and science till

---

* As a friendly critic, Mr Paul Segal, has rightly pointed out, I here tacitly assume the correctness of logical positivism without subjecting it to the same kind of psycho-analytical examination as I have attempted in the case of classical philosophy. I agree with him that in its early days, logical positivism was by no means free from emotional bias (splitting), classical philosophy being its 'bad' object and physics its over-idealised 'good' one.

comparatively recent times. Then they made up for the delay by producing men like Spinoza in philosophy and Freud or Einstein in science.

Meanwhile it was the early philosophers of Greece who first had the courage to face the mysterious dangers of cosmic and moral speculation. And the risks were not altogether fanciful. For if the gods themselves did not exact the expected punishment, the faithful were apt to exact it on their behalf. Indeed, from Socrates onwards, philosophy has always had its martyrs. But to the unconscious mind, I think, the imaginary dangers were always greater than the real ones, and the fear of these can still be an unseen impediment to curiosity about ultimate things which perhaps stand for the first things the child was aggressively curious about.

I would tentatively suggest that science, in later separating itself from philosophy, also freed itself from some of these unconscious anxieties, and that it did so by means of a partial renunciation. This renunciation can be overt, as for example when a scientist leaves all 'ultimate questions' to religion, and confines his curiosity to what he may think of as the material world. But I believe a similar renunciation can occur unconsciously, even when it appears not to have been made at all. He may assert, for example, that all significant questions can be answered in principle by science, and that such metaphysical questions as appear to be unanswerable result from bad grammar and are not significant. This may be sound logic, but, psychologically, it suggests a sour-grape attitude towards some kind of ultimate knowledge which is renounced, though still unconsciously desired. Perhaps, therefore, what was specific to philosophical curiosity was that it retained more of its original aim—the pursuit of a knowledge felt, in some sense, to be ultimate; and we may add total as opposed to piecemeal. But this does not explain why such knowledge was to be obtained by contemplation, by looking inwards rather than at the external world; nor why the quest should be illogical, as the critics claim it to have been, as if it contained some inner contradiction.

The characteristic of looking inwards to discover the

secrets of the universe would seem to imply that the osten-
sible object of speculation, the cosmos, was felt to mirror, or to
be mirrored by, an inner world of absorbing interest. Moreover, there was a perfectionist element in past philosophical
activity which seems related more to art than science, and
suggests that curiosity was, after all, of secondary importance
—that the ultimate aim was less to know, than to create, the
universe. Psychologically, such an aim is less absurd than it
may seem. For what to an outside observer is our picture,
or model, of the world is to us the very world itself. In this
sense we can create it. And we can do so in many ways
—for example, teleologically or mechanistically. And the
apparent contradiction between two ways need not be real.
If both correspond with experience at every point at which
they can be tested, they represent the same phenomena—
like two equations of a curve, one in cartesian, the other in
polar, co-ordinates. (This was the theme of the first paper I
ever published (3).)

But though the world can be conceived in many different
ways, the common-sense picture of it most of us employ is not
particularly original. It is influenced by, and largely copied
from, that which is current in our time. And once completed,
we seldom question it again. The philosopher is different in
that he creates what others copy. Indeed, his determination
to create would seem to imply a refusal to copy which may be
linked with that contempt for observation of which the classical philosophers have often been accused. Hegel, for example, when told that history did not conform to his philosophy, is reported to have said, 'So much the worse for
history'. Such denial of facts, combined as it is with great
creative ability, can express, I think, an unconscious envy
of the parental gods, whose work is so much admired that it
has to be ignored and re-created (4). What, of course, was
ignored, or actively destroyed and re-created, was, not the
universe as made by God, but the old models of it made by
previous philosophers—especially that enshrined in common-
sense philosophy. And what, in the end, was so much admired as the work of God was the work of the philosopher

who created the new model—and this may really have been an intellectual achievement of the highest order.

The two motives so far discussed—a curiosity and a creativeness which express an unconscious challenge to parents, whose creativity may consciously remain the object of grateful admiration—could partially explain the demand for total as opposed to piece-meal knowledge, and the refusal to look for it outside. In some degree, too, the will to create rather than to copy could explain why many philosophers have condemned classical philosophy as futile; for, if science is right, the secrets of the universe are only discoverable by observation. But this does not solve what according to the critics is the greatest puzzle: that the basic aim of classical philosophy—the pursuit of synthetic *a priori* knowledge—was not merely futile, like looking in the wrong place for something, but illogical, like looking for a round square.

Perhaps we can get a little further if we examine a third motive for philosophy, and that is doubt. Philosophical doubt has become proverbial. What others take for granted, whether in morals or in the theory of reality, arouses doubt in the philosopher, and this may well be his initial motive. It should be confessed at once that doubt applied to the philosophy of common sense is often justified. For if the lay-man examines his own philosophy, he will probably find it to be full of inconsistencies. It may contain, for example, different codes of ethics—one for home, one for the office, perhaps another for Sundays, and two more for domestic and foreign politics—as well as different theories of reality, one materialistic and another theological.

Now, these discordant elements express different and incompatible aspects of personality, which co-exist peacefully enough only because they seldom meet. We are accustomed to associate splitting mechanisms with schizophrenia, but they are also the means by which ordinary people defend themselves against the anxieties aroused by internal conflicts. The hedonic gain is obvious if conflicting attitudes to the same thing at the same time can be replaced by different attitudes to different things at different times; and this is what splitting achieves—though at the cost of truth. I believe one of the main characteristics of the classical philosopher was that such evasion of conflict by means of a little splitting, which comes so easily to most of us, was very hard for him. For this reason, he started more conscious of inconsistencies in his initial picture of the world, and therefore more troubled by doubts which reflected his greater awareness of ambivalence. Simultaneously to satisfy both sides of any conflict, rather than to satisfy each separately by splitting, may have been the source of the illogical aim he is accused of.

I think he often did achieve a higher degree of integration, of harmony of system, than other people; but the essential inconsistencies of human nature would seem to preclude complete success. At any rate, it is perhaps doubtful whether a philosophical system which is both internally consistent and comprehensive has ever been created. Most classical systems have been shown by other philosophers, either to be self-contradictory after all, or to have gained their consistency at the cost of leaving something out which ought to be in, but is not in because it will not fit. Such defects are usually attributed to the immense complexity of the task. But they may also reflect essential inconsistencies in man which no system can resolve.* What at first sight may appear as an unusually harmonious personality, with no minor splits, is sometimes achieved at the cost of a major split elsewhere which involves the total exclusion of an important aspect of the self. And I think the same thing can happen to a philosophic system. As far as it goes, it may be a completely harmonious picture of the world; but some whole section of what ordinary people call reality—it may be matter or mind, or perhaps the concept of evil—is ignored.

I would stress that much of what I have just said is neces-

---

* I wish to imply, not that it is logically impossible to construct a system which, within its own level, is consistent and comprehensive, but that it may be psychologically impossible to achieve the hidden aim of complete self-integration by means of the construction of such a system.

sarily speculative. But at least we have some theories to test against examples.

Doubt and Certainty in Ethics

That the stimulus to ethical inquiry comes from moral doubts and conflicts within the self seems highly probable. Those who 'know what is right' are not aware of any problem, though to others they may seem to have shelved rather than to have solved it. In contrast to people of this kind, the philosopher of morals is more likely to be found among those who, having lost faith in the code they started with, are in search of a consistent alternative. Our problem is to trace these doubts to their origin.

To the psycho-analyst, the first step at least seems comparatively easy. Everyone is by now familiar with Freud's explanation of conscience: that it begins with the child's fear of displeasing his parents and reaches its final form when he 'introjects' them, or rather his ideas of them, as far stricter and 'better' than they really were. But because this idea of an internal authority, or super-ego to give it Freud's term, is largely unconscious, it is to this extent unalterable, so that the conscious ego, which does develop and mature, may become increasingly in conflict with it. The initial impulse to ethical inquiry may well come from conflicts of this kind, and end in one of two ways: either the authority of the super-ego is bolstered up by the construction of systems that purport to be absolute, or undermined by a scepticism designed to rob it of its terrors. Kant's ethics, with its stress on the categorical imperative, would seem a good example of the first alternative; that of the Epicureans, who attacked superstition as the cause of fear, a good example of the second.

But below such ego-super-ego conflicts is another which is, I think, more fundamental. Freud's theory of a conflict between life and death instincts is still controversial among analysts themselves; and of those who accept it, some do so with reservations and others with additions. Thus, while Freud believed in a death instinct but not in a basic fear of death, Melanie Klein believes in both. Personally, I find the concept of a death instinct difficult. But I believe in innate destructive impulses which necessarily have the, at first solipsistic, self as their primary object, and so give rise to the fear of death. In a form which is relevant to ethics, I would put it thus : deep in the unconscious, the ultimate source of anxiety is our own aggression, especially aggressive greed, which, however, may seem to threaten us, either from within* or from without, like a foreign force. Then, as a defence against the resulting unconscious intensification of the fear of death, the aggressive component in the ego's will to live may be increased to such a degree that every external object tends to be unconsciously viewed as a kind of nourishment to be consumed or as a threat to be destroyed. But, in conflict with this completely predatory egoism, the ego has developed an opposite tendency to embrace and identify itself with other objects, which it then as desperately endeavours to preserve. So an insoluble unconscious conflict threatens to arise, and is averted in the first place largely by mechanisms of splitting which tend to divide the world into enemies to be destroyed and friends to be protected from the external replicas of our own aggression.

This solution, maintained as it is by some denial of unlikeable qualities in the friends and of likeable ones in the enemies, is stable only so long as it is not too closely examined. Those who do examine it, if only semi-consciously, may be faced with the ethical problem in what I think is its most basic form: whether to prey on others that we may thrive or to sacrifice ourselves that they may.† Of course the dichotomy is not so absolute as it appears to the unconscious, for our interests and those of others are often the same. But to a great extent an incompatibility of interests, and indeed a

* Thus, for example, we speak of hunger 'gnawing' as if it were a devouring enemy inside.

† Freud speaks of 'a carrying-over into the region of the mind of the dilemma—eat or be eaten—which dominates the organic world' ('Anxiety and Instinctual Life' in *New Introductory Lectures on Psycho-Analysis*, 1933).

competition for survival, does in fact exist. The classical philosopher would seem to have been, at least pre-consciously, more aware of this dichotomy than others. Perhaps he also unconsciously exaggerated it.

The underlying problem of how to thrive without feeling guilty at doing so at the expense of others is primarily internal. Most philosophers have treated it as such; but some have sought to evade it by treating it as solely external. Rousseau, for example, blamed society for all our faults and tried to construct an ideal one in which we should all be good as well as happy. He substituted, as it were, a myth of primal innocence for that of original sin. Thus his system was achieved at the cost of leaving something out—namely, the whole problem of the individual's sense of guilt which is rooted in ambivalence. We can give him credit for helping to inspire those liberal movements which really reduced some social tensions and so lessened one external cause of internal conflict. But the consistent development of his denial of the individual's unconscious sense of responsibility for predatory aggression led in the end, not to the emancipation of individuals from their sense of guilt, but to the mass projection of conscience, in its most ferocious form, into totalitarian states which sought to control even the thoughts of individuals.

I do not wish to imply that the attempt to improve the external world is necessarily futile. But I do think that past attempts to do so have been disappointing. Those two dominant expressions of our innate aggressiveness, greed and envy, do not seem to diminish in proportion to a reduction in their apparent external causes. And the unconscious guilt they arouse remains a secret motive for a demand for scapegoats. It looks as if these impulses might have to be diminished through a better understanding of ourselves before the benefits of a more humane society can be fully realised.

In contrast to Rousseau, Kant was concerned to devise, or, as he thought, to discover, a universal code for individuals. According to his 'categorical imperative', we ought each to act in such a way that we could wish our own behaviour to become a general law governing the behaviour of everyone. Philosophically considered, I do not think, as he did, that this is a synthetic judgment *a priori*. But as a contribution to the psychological problem of achieving an optimum compromise between egoism and altruism, it would seem to have much to recommend it.

It is characteristic of philosophers, who demand consistency, that they are not content with a merely personal solution of the moral problem. Their aim is to find some one standard which everyone has only to understand to agree to. If there can be no such things as synthetic judgments *a priori*, the quest may seem a vain one, and, for this reason, the ethical relativists have abandoned it as hopeless. But I think there is a sense in which it may, after all, be partially achieved. Since Plato there has been, as it were, a persistent hunch among philosophers that wickedness is the result of ignorance, and that if we were all wise we should all be good; and by this is implied good according to some universally accepted standard. Now, if by wisdom we understand knowledge of ourselves, there is much recent analytic evidence that different people in fact approximate to a common type of moral character, which I have called humanist, as they advance in this kind of knowledge. In other words, the hunch about a common standard for all wise men, which so many philosophers have tried to prove by non-empirical arguments, begins to seem probable in the light of recent empirical discoveries—a theme which I have developed elsewhere (5).

The Theory of Reality

Turning from ethics to the theory of reality, the same passion for consistency is responsible for much which to the ordinary man seems palpably absurd. And, as before, the initial motive is doubt, this time directed towards the physical aspect of our common-sense picture of the world.

Take, for instance, the theory of reality as developed by Locke, Berkeley, and Hume. From the beginning, philosophers have been troubled by doubts aroused by apparent inconsistencies between what things seem to be and what they are. When the end of a stick is dipped in water, it looks bent. The ordinary man is not much troubled by such experiences. The stick looks bent but he 'knows' it is really straight and can 'prove' this by feeling it. The philosopher is less easily content. 'If', he will say, 'my sense of sight can deceive me, why should I be more sure that my sense of touch is telling me the truth? How, in fact, can I be sure that all my senses are not deceiving me with an "appearance" (hallucination?) totally unlike reality?'* Or, to put the question in another way: 'Are there any qualities which I can attribute to the "real" stick as opposed to those I can attribute to its appearance?' To this question common sense before the time of Locke would probably have answered that the colour belongs to the appearance and the hardness to the reality. Locke argued that there is no essential difference between the two, and that the hardness, the 'feel of' the stick, like its colour, is a sensual or subjective quality and belongs to the appearance. But as opposed to these secondary qualities, substantiality and extension belong, he said, to the 'real' objective thing. This division, which for a long time was good enough for science, still influences our common-sense conception of the world. But, in fact, Berkeley soon showed it to be entirely artificial. For, like colour, hardness, and so forth, substantiality and extension are perceptible qualities, though terminologically disguised, and belong to the appearance; so the whole distinction between appearance and reality, in this sense, disappears. To be consistent, therefore, Berkeley thought of objects as being real only when perceived, and as existing only in the minds of their percipients. This, of course, threatened to leave him with a very discontinuous world, in which objects existed only intermittently. But he saved the situation with the aid of God, who is always perceiving everything, and so keeps it permanently real. It remained for the agnostic Hume

* However valuable in philosophy, a doubt of this kind has unmistakable affinities with the distrust of the paranoid who, because of his own ambivalence, is unable to trust any other person.

cheerfully to remove the final prop, and to leave us, as it were, floating in a purely subjective world. In his philosophy, not only do objects consist only of their secondary qualities and therefore exist only when perceived, but we ourselves consist only of our sensations and our thoughts, and therefore exist only when awake. In Hume's view this is the only consistent way of thinking of the world. But he admitted that neither he nor anyone else could think consistently for any length of time.

Our psychological problem is to discover whether this is another case of consistency being achieved at the cost of leaving something out which ought to be in. What is, of course, left out is the concept of a substance, or matter, which can exist without being perceived. To both Berkeley and Hume such a concept is self-contradictory. As psychologists, we want to discover whether this was their sole objection to it, or whether for some other reason it aroused an unconscious animus in them.

In the case of Berkeley, at least, there are some grounds for supposing that it did. For J. O. Wisdom (6), in a recent book, has argued that to Berkeley, who in the end became hypochondriacally preoccupied with purging his own body, the very idea of matter had a persecutory significance and, as such, had to be eliminated from his picture of the world. No one, as far as I know, has attempted a similar analysis in the case of Hume, who appears to have been one of the sanest, as well as one of the most amiable, of men. But we do know that the force of his own logic led him to construct a picture of the world so strange and so repugnant to common sense that he himself could never hold it for any length of time. And what, I think, his logic did lead him to construct, or reconstruct, was the phenomenological world of the infant from which the common-sense picture is developed.

But whether Hume's philosophy was or was not influenced, in any great degree, by unconscious motives, the resistance to it certainly was. We take our common-sense picture of the world too much for granted, and so forget that it is a picture created by ourselves. Moreover, it can be lost or destroyed in certain states of madness, in which it can, as it were, disintegrate into its original elements, and so lose its comforting solidity. It is, I think, the fear of this disaster that Hume's philosophy so greatly stirred—a fear which Dr Johnson eloquently expressed when he stamped on the pavement to prove that it was real.

The Construction of World Models

This brings me to the contribution of philosophy to psychoanalysis. If we are not all philosophers, there is an important sense in which we all have a philosophy—that is, a general picture of the world—together with general rules of conduct. Thus the current philosophy of common sense is what a philosopher would call a naïve dualism. To the psychic part belong our sensations, thoughts, and feelings, perhaps also an anthropomorphic concept of a psyche, mind, or soul which 'owns' them, and is itself saddled with a conscience. To the physical part belong the physical objects we 'perceive' and think of as ultimately analysable into non-perceptible molecules, atoms, electrons, and so on. (See also (7).)

Subjectivist philosophers, like Hume and his successors, Mach and Avenarius, have taught us not to take this common-sense world for granted. They have also constructed a monistic and subjective alternative which, at least in its cognitive aspect, is probably quite close to the world of the infant. By so doing they raised the psychologically important problem of how one is developed from the other. And I think that that branch of philosophy which is concerned with logic and the construction of language may have given us the outline of a model which may aid the solution of the problem.

The main difficulty in the subjectivist point of view is that most presentations of it do not make adequate provision for the concept of linguistic symbolism and external reference. If all the qualities of a perceived object are subjective, the object as a transcendental entity does not exist. But applying the same argument to a remembered object, we might arrive at the conclusion that all its qualities belong to our *present* subjective experience, and that the past perception, of which it is the memory, does not exist. And this comes perilously near to the assertion that, since there is nothing, we cannot think of anything beyond our momentary experience; in other words, that ideas have no external reference and language, whether verbal or non-verbal, no meaning.

So what the extreme subjectivist seems to be depicting is the momentary world of a person who has no language, not even a language of pre-verbal thought, with which to refer to the objects of memory or expectation. Now, this does seem to approximate, though only in its cognitive aspect, to the world of the infant. For at the beginning memories and expectations, which later have external reference, are not yet differentiated from phantasies so charged with emotion that they have a hallucinatory vividness which makes them indistinguishable from perceptions.

But even the emergence of the distinction between present thought and its absent object, which enables the more integrated child to think of a permanent world, is probably not alone sufficient to enable him to think of a dualistic one. For to do this, he must not only be able to think and feel about permanent, as distinct from intermittent, objects, but also to identify with others and become able to think and feel, from an outside point of view—that is, self-consciously—about the relation of his own thought and feelings to them. The intermediate stage, of being able to think of permanent objects but not of the relation of the thought itself to them, reminds me of a limitation of language first pointed out by Witgenstein, which Russell showed how to circumvent (8). According to Witgenstein, no language can express its own relation to what it represents. So that, according to Russell, if we do talk about this relation we must do so in a language of a higher order than the first. Of course it is difficult to say when the capacity to use a second-order language begins, especially as it is at first a language of pre-verbal thought. But its emergence would seem to be equivalent to the emergence of a capacity to identify ourselves with others, and so to think and feel, self-consciously, that is, from outside, about the relation of our thoughts and feelings to their objects. And this in turn would seem to be equivalent to the emergence of a dualistic picture of the world.

To the philosophers, therefore, we owe not only our first awareness of there being a problem about the development of our dualistic picture of the world, but also the suggestion of there being at least three stages in this development, which correspond with no language, first-order language, and second-order language. It remains for psychology to fill in the details.

This can be attempted by two independent methods: by the direct observation of children and by the psycho-analysis of children and adults. The first is used by Jean Piaget in his important work *The Child's Construction of Reality* (1955). I must leave it to others to correlate the observational and the psycho-analytic approach. My present aim is only to correlate the philosophical and the analytic one.

Stages of Development

In other words, I shall try to combine the cognitive stages suggested by philosophy with the emotional stages, or positions, reconstructed by analysis. In doing so, I have been guided, in the main, by Melanie Klein's discoveries (9). B t I have also borrowed concepts from biology. The result is a five-stage model of development, the first three of which more or less correspond with the 'no language' stage suggested by subjectivist philosophy. I should add that my reconstruction does not claim to be more than tentative. It is also artificially schematic.

The first post-natal stage, just after what Freud described as the 'shock' of birth, is probably akin to the buzzing confusion imagined by William James; though we believe we can add that it is a persecutory confusion of a traumatic kind. Probably this is soon followed—perhaps within hours—by a stage in which certain *Gestalten*, or significant patterns of sensation, begin to emerge. We know from such students of animal behaviour as Tinbergen (10) and Lorenz (11), that certain patterns of stimuli evoke innate responses, for ex-

ample, in newly hatched birds. And we have reason to
believe this to be true also of the human infant. Moreover,
just as the newly hatched gull responds by gaping to a red
spot on cardboard in the same way as it would to the red
spot on its mother's bill, so the human infant may not at
first discriminate between different members of a class of
objects having the same *Gestalt*—that, for example, of a
breast. Nor does he distinguish between the percept and the
hallucinatory memory of it.

We must try, then, to envisage this second stage as one in
which there is little or no symbolism in either of two important senses. There is no symbolism in what may be broadly
called the linguistic sense, because the idea, for example of the
breast, has the hallucinatory vividness of a percept, and so
cannot yet stand *for* past or future percepts not present at the
time. For this reason, the 'object' has an intermittent rather
than a permanent or 'objective' existence. And there is little
symbolism even in the psycho-analytic sense. What we later
call symbols are, rather, equated with their objects (12); for
no one member of the class of patterns having the same
Gestalt, and evoking an innate response, is yet clearly distinguished as *the* object of which the other members later
become symbols eliciting only a partial response. Nevertheless, there is one sense in which these *Gestalten* may be said to
be significant: the baby behaves 'as if' he recognised them
as objects of intense desire, or of destructive hatred and
persecutory fear.

It is, in fact, these different affective responses which determine the only discrimination made at this stage: that between
good or pleasurable and bad or painful experience. And this
distinction cuts right through later identities. For the various
appearances, whether sensed or hallucinated, of what will
later be thought of as one object are at first classified into
two groups, one good and beneficent, the other bad and
persecutory. Sometimes the good, sometimes the bad, aspect
comes into being and then ceases to exist; for they are not
yet thought of as continuing to exist when neither hallucinated nor perceived.

The third stage in my over-schematic presentation is that in which one only of the members of a class of patterns having the same *Gestalt* elicits a total response, while the response to the others becomes partial. That is to say, they become symbols in the psycho-analytic sense. They can be *substitutes* for what we should call the real object; but they do not yet *represent* it in the way that an idea, or later a word, can represent an absent object. By this time the good and bad aspects of the same object have different symbols; and, since good symbols tend to become bad whenever they arouse anger or fear, they are continually being replaced by new ones. In this way the infant's world is rapidly enriched. But although it has many 'objects' in it, these are not yet 'objective' in the sense of being substantial and permanent.

Up to this point, therefore, the infant's philosophy is a subjective monism, akin to that of Hume—though it is emotionally split into good and bad. Only in the next or fourth stage, when 'good' and 'bad' phantasies become more integrated and so lose some of their hallucinatory intensity, can they acquire 'meaning' as referring to percepts which are 'external' in that they are not being actually perceived. Then, while much of phantasy remains an unconscious part of an immanent subjective world, conscious imagery emerges from it to form the thought-model of an external objective world which, unlike Berkeley's, continues to exist even when not observed. In other words, the child has a first-order language of pre-verbal conscious thought with which to make a model of experience. But his world is not yet fully dualistic. A subjective monism has been replaced by a predominantly monistic materialism; for although he now thinks of an external world in relation to himself, he does not yet think with full self-consciousness of his mental ego's relation to it.

Only in the final stage—and I would remind you again that I am describing a fluctuating process as if it occurred in steps—does the child more definitely project his observing self, at first into his parents—that is, identify himself with them—and so observe, as it were from without, his own emotional relation to them and to the external world in general.

From the beginning there has been an interplay between what we call 'introjective' and 'projective' mechanisms. And this implies that there has been some boundary, and a fluctuating one, between what is at first mainly a 'body-ego', controlled by phantasies, emotions and unconscious processes, and more objective perceptions. But what can belong alternately to the self or to the external world in earlier stages is not an integrated ego—and still less a self-conscious one. In these earlier stages it is, I think, more the primitive *Gestalten*, endowed with the simple affects of love, hate, or fear they arouse, that could at one moment be 'introjected' to form part of the self and at the next 'projected' outside. Moreover, at first the aim of these mechanisms was only, on the one hand, to get rid of, and ultimately to annihilate, all bad objects and feelings, and on the other to assimilate all the good ones into the self—in short, to preserve a blissful solipsism, all good, all one, all self. This, incidentally, would seem to be the aim of certain mystical philosophies. But in the stage we are now trying to reconstruct, introjection and projection are being used in a more complex way to form the concepts of one's own and other people's minds.

It would be difficult to say which comes first. For the two ideas seem to develop together and to enrich each other. But I will suppose that, as soon as objects come to be thought of as having a permanent existence, the former simple affective response to them develops into more complex sentiments, each of which might constitute a kind of part ego. Such a sentiment, once formed, can then be projected into, or attributed to, its object—for example, the mother—no longer to get rid of it if it is bad, but also to endow her with goodness if it is good. Moreover, it is felt to be expressed in her behaviour which can thus confirm and enrich it. In other words, his picture of her sentiment, originally based on identification, is more realistically developed. And then, by imitating, or reintrojecting his picture of her, his picture of his own mental self is in turn enriched. So, by an alternating process of introjection and projection, the concepts of his own and other people's egos are gradually built up.

This stage in which the child learns to think of himself and others as people, with similar feelings and desires, is the one in which he begins to feel concerned for them, and for himself, as people—in particular, concerned for the damage he may do them in imagination when he is angry. In fact, the most important turning-point in his early development is reached, the 'depressive position' discovered and so termed by Melanie Klein, when he is capable of being deterred, not merely by anxieties of a persecutory kind but by feelings of guilt. And from now on he is a moral being, with a moral conflict between love and hate and between egoism and altruism.

But the aspect of this stage I would emphasise here is the child's greater capacity to identify with others, and so view, as it were from without, his own feelings in their relation to objects—to be self-consciously conscious of experience. To the infant, and in unself-conscious periods to the adult as well, perception, filled out by memory beyond the field of view, constitutes or *is* the world. But as soon as he can split off part of his observing self outside, this complex of perception and memory which a moment ago was the objective world itself, becomes a subjective picture of it. Such a momentous change in outlook is, I have argued, equivalent to the acquisition of a second-order language—a second-order thought-model of the world—which is dualistic because its object is the relation of mind to matter in the broadest sense.

Although I believe that the five stages I have described do roughly correspond to significant points in a developmental process, which ends in the dualistic philosophy of common sense, I do not wish to imply that there are only five or that they can all be clearly distinguished. The main ones can be. Others are inserted because they seem to be almost logically required—like the intermediate steps in an argument of which we are given only the beginning and the end.

Moreover, the last stage would seem to be at least intermittently reached, though not consolidated, at a very early age, after which there are only refinements to be made. For there is a good deal of evidence that the depressive position is reached about the middle of the first half-year, and this I think implies that the child, if only pre-consciously, can identify himself sufficiently with his mother to begin to imagine his own relation to her from her point of view. If so, he already has the essential rudiments of a second-order thought-model of the world, although he has not yet acquired a verbal language and is still incapable of verbal thought.

Language and Verbal Thought

Pure imagery, without the use of words, is thus, I think, sufficient to form, not only a first-order model but also a second-order one, and so to achieve the dualistic philosophy of common sense. But all the refinements in these models, which distinguish us from our pre-verbal ancestors, potentially perhaps no less intelligent, are the product of language in the narrow sense, and of the capacity for verbal thought.

Verbal language, which Hobbes called the greatest invention of all other, presupposes an imagery based largely on psycho-analytic symbols in a way first described by Ernest Jones (13). But in the end this imagery is restricted to verbal signs, linked only by custom to what they represent. Of its many functions we are here concerned only with its use in recording and extending knowledge by the construction of word-models of the expected possibilities of experience. In accordance with the dualistic nature of the overriding model, knowledge is of three kinds: psychological, physical, and psycho-physical. It is on the role of language in psychological knowledge that I would like to conclude.

Psychology is in a sense a very ancient science. At least from the time when language acquired proper names, personal pronouns, and verbs to express emotions and other mental states, man has been, if intermittently, raising the level of his own self-consciousness—a form of progress which perhaps best deserves the name.

The chief credit for the advances of the past is due to the

poets who, even before writing was invented, have been creating imaginary characters, personifying traits, which their hearers could then for the first time apprehend and recognise as existing in those around them or in themselves. Everyone, for example, is now familiar with Shakespeare's main characters. They have become part of our understanding of psychology because he created them. By doing so he raised self-consciousness and intuition to an appreciably higher level than it was before.

The philosophers, too, have done the same, though in their case it was more the intellectual than the emotional and unconscious aspect of our psychology that their work has helped us the better to perceive. To them we owe much of our knowledge of how we form at least the intellectual part of our picture of the world.

Moreover, this work of the poets and philosophers, so far as it has increased self-consciousness and intuition by putting into words so many states of mind which otherwise would have remained unnoticed, has to this extent already mastered some part of the unconscious. So psychology and psycho-analysis have ancient forerunners. What is new in it is the explicit recognition of unconscious processes and the development of a specialised technique for their exploration. This is the achievement of Freud.

It may be expected that, with the aid of this new technique, there will be an acceleration in the rate at which the level of consciousness, and so also the sense of personal responsibility, is raised. Something of the kind has already taken place. We cannot yet judge its full significance. But if the new insights are not lost in some calamity, the future historian may well look back on Freud's work as marking a decisive change in the tempo of human progress.

BIBLIOGRAPHY

(1) WITGENSTEIN, Tractatus Logico Philosophicus, 1922.
(2) See KLEIN, MELANIE, Contributions to Psycho-Analysis, 1948, especially the paper on Intellectual Inhibitions (1931).

(3) MONEY-KYRLE, R., 'Belief and Representation', which appeared in the first and only volume of *Symposion*, 1925–6.

(4) KLEIN, MELANIE, 'A Study in Envy and Gratitude.' Read at the 1955 International Congress of Psycho-Analysis, and shortly to be published as a book.

(5) MONEY-KYRLE, R., 'Psycho-Analysis and Ethics', 1952; (republished in *New Directions in Psycho-Analysis*, 1955) and, *Psycho-Analysis and Politics*, 1951.

(6) WISDOM, J. O. (1953). *Unconscious Origin of Berkeley's Philosophy*. London: Hogarth Press.

(7) MONEY-KYRLE, R., 'The World of the Unconscious and the World of Common Sense', *British Journal for the Philosophy of Science*, VII, 25, 1956.

(8) See Russell's Introduction to the English Translation of Witgenstein's *Tractatus*.

(9) See KLEIN, MELANIE, *The Psycho-Analysis of Children*, 1932; *Contributions to Psycho-Analysis*, 1948; as well as the papers by herself and her colleagues in *Developments in Psycho-Analysis*, 1952, and *New Directions in Psycho-Analysis*, 1955.

(10) TINBERGEN, *The Study of Instinct*, 1951.

(11) LORENZ, *King Solomon's Ring*, 1952.

(12) KLEIN, MELANIE, 'The Importance of Symbol Formation in the Development of the Ego', *Contributions to Psycho-Analysis*, 1948.
SEGAL, H., Paper on 'Symbol Formation' to be published shortly.

(13) JONES, ERNEST, 'The Theory of Symbolism', *Papers on Psycho-Analysis*, 1918.

VI

PSYCHO-ANALYSIS AND THE CURRENT ECONOMIC CRISIS

By Elliott Jaques, m.a., m.d., ph.d.

The centenary of Sigmund Freud comes at a time of perplexing economic uncertainty. We have the spectacle of apparently irrational and self-destructive economic impulses at work causing inflation. This state of affairs would surely have attracted Freud's scientific attention. Despite government exhortation, wage spiralling continues. And despite the fact that each wage increase no longer means any very real consequent gain in standard of living, there is no immediate sign of abatement of wage pressure.

One of the very important factors causing self-control of our economic relations to elude us is the perpetual conflict between rival wage-earning groups and between economic classes. The outcome of this conflict is to restore an unrecognised and unspecified, but nevertheless very delicate, balance in the level of our money-incomes relative to each other. The potency of this rivalry between us, arising in one region after another because of repeated disturbances in the pattern of real money differentials between groups, has become a menace to our economic survival.

I wish this evening to show how the work of Freud—and the scientific development he set in train through his successors—is directly and urgently relevant to the resolution of our current economic and industrial dilemma. The attempt to apply Freud's work in this way need occasion no surprise. In his wide-ranging studies, Freud went well beyond the subject of emotional disturbance in the individual, applying himself to the analysis and understanding of the play of unconscious factors in group psychology. Group rivalry on a scale approaching self-destructiveness is a theme at the heart of psycho-analytic endeavour. And when this group rivalry is concerned with economic and material security and gain, then it may seem self-evident that powerful unconscious forces are likely to be at work.

Our Unconscious Evaluation of Our Work

It is a bitter paradox that our recent years of peace-time full employment—the first such years in the modern history of our nation—have been attended by calamitous disputes over payment.

What is required for balance and self-control to be regained is a structure of payment which would assure to each of us a return for our work in line with the responsibility we carry. So long as we each received comparable payment for comparable responsibility, the problem of differentials would be diminished and possibly resolved. Such a view is widely accepted in theory. Agreement upon this goal of economic fairness and equity is, however, much easier to realise than agreement upon the means of achieving the goal.

The problem of resolving the acute rivalries stimulated by payment differentials is commonly regarded as intractable. We are each of us prone to regard the other as out to get just as much as he can. Greedy self-interest is supposed to have supplanted a responsible giving of fair work in return for one's pay. Interest and satisfaction in doing a good job are presumed to have been lost. Supply and demand are held to rule the labour market—shortages of some types of skill supposedly allowing those in possession of those skills to hold the community to ransom for excessive incomes solely because of scarcity.

Our psycho-analytic experience would warn us, however, not to accord too ready acceptance to these commonly held views. I propose to suggest to you that an orderly pattern of behaviour can be scientifically observed within the apparent disarray and jumble of our procedures for regulating payment and work in industry; that there is, in fact, a systematic national wage and salary scale which is unconsciously perceived, understood, and, most important, put to use; and that we are each well aware, unconsciously, not only of our own true level of capacity for work, but also to what extent we are being accorded responsibility consistent with our capacity, and payment consistent with that responsibility within the national scale of earning. This is not to say that we always behave in accord with our unconscious awareness of this reality, and that we never behave irrationally or neurotically.

At the same time, I shall endeavour to show how a gross denial, constituting a sort of psycho-pathology on a national scale—a mass psychotic process in which we all unconsciously participate—inhibits scientific recognition of these realities of work relationships and of individual motivation. It may, then, be possible to demonstrate that some of our general conceptions about economic behaviour are themselves the projection of our own unconscious motives—a projection caused by unconscious anxieties which make us blind to the most commonplace and ubiquitous characteristics of everyday social and economic relationships.

The Normal Earning Growth Curve

If we study the pattern of real earnings of individuals, a certain regularity may be observed. By real earnings is meant a person's money income corrected for changes in the national wages index. A curve of earnings can be found for each person (employed in industry) which commonly shows a regular progression. These curves are shown in the first diagram (Fig. 18) of the real earnings of some 100 individuals employed in industry. If we examine the general pattern of these curves, we see that there is a general trend—that they arrange themselves like iron filings on a paper over a magnet. The curves conforming to this regular pattern I shall call *normal earning growth curves*, for reasons which I shall describe. Their shape is that of typical biological growth curves.

The most striking and, perhaps, unexpected regularities are found when we consider our intuitive and unerring judgment of our own earning growth curves. Conformance of our

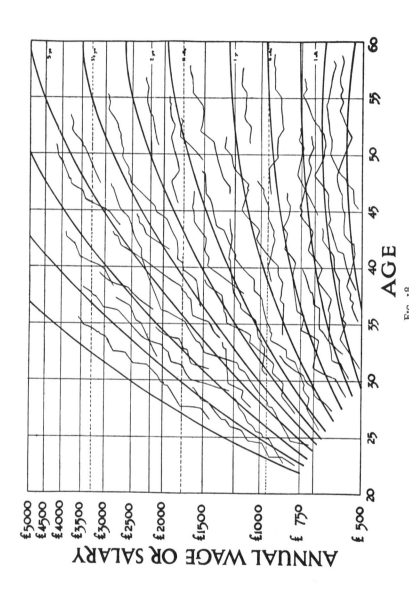

Fig. 18.

earnings to a normal curve is accompanied by the sense that we are getting a proper income within the current payment levels. More may be desired, but nevertheless we experience a sense of fair pay for our worth relative to others.

Deviations from this regular progression are experienced as follows. Deviation upwards feels like being overpaid relative to others. When overpayment of this kind is experienced for any length of time, guilt and anxiety set in. Compulsive expenditure with purchasing characterised by waste and ugliness ensues—expenditure described by the economist as naïve ostentation beyond the norm of conspicuous consumption. Or an equally compulsive hoarding may occur.

Deviation downwards (the most common circumstance in an inflationary economy) is accompanied by a sense of underpayment. Poor morale is to be found under these circumstances, with symptoms ranging from anger and disaffection with pressure for increase in pay, to depressed acceptance of the situation and feelings of worthlessness.

These symptoms are quite familiar and have been known throughout time. Plato, for instance, complains : 'There seem to be two causes of the deterioration of the arts—wealth and poverty. Wealth is the parent of luxury and indolence, poverty of meanness and viciousness, and both of discontent.'

Our intuitive response to deviations from our expected earning level can be precisely observed. Deviations of two per cent are just noticed. Deviations above ten per cent evoke strong feelings, and the impulse to leave one's job. And if you ask a man to state what he thinks he will be earning in, say, five years' time, he will name a figure remarkably close to that to be concluded by extrapolating his earning growth curve. His prediction is unaffected by whether or not he might be considered financially ambitious. The same conformance appears in the man who says he needs to gain more money and the man who says money is not of much importance to him.

These observations are illustrated in the accompanying

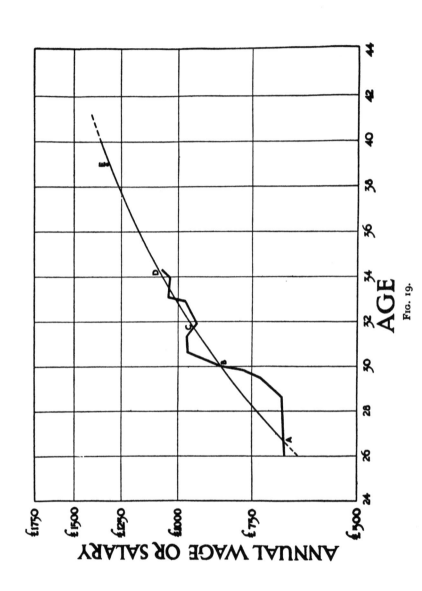

ANNUAL WAGE OR SALARY

£1750
£1500
£1250
£1000
£750
£500

24 26 28 30 32 34 36 38 40 42 44

AGE

FIG. 19.

diagram (Fig. 19). This is the actual corrected earning curve of one individual who has authorised me to use it. Between A and B he felt underpaid—becoming resentful until his real earnings began to climb again. He and his wife experienced great difficulty in sustaining their standard of living. Between B and C he felt overpaid—becoming rather contemptuous because he was getting away with something, and mildly ashamed. Neither he nor his wife considered the amount above the dotted line as money to be budgeted for. It was something extra, spent on they were not quite sure what. When at C this extra amount was no longer forthcoming, their standard of living was not felt to have fallen. Between C and D a state of relative equilibrium was experienced. He said that in order to be satisfied he would expect his earnings to have increased to E in five years' time. He was confident they would. These feelings were, of course, described before he knew anything whatsoever about normal earning growth curves. This example is one instance of what has become my repeated experience.

You may have noted that I have so far avoided one question of particular importance: How has the relevant earning growth curve been selected? Might not the expected curve be above that drawn, so that payment had been consistently low? Or might it not be below that drawn, so that payment had been consistently high?

In recent work, which I have described elsewhere (1), I have presented the following findings and conclusions. The level of work a man carries in his job—in the sense of size of responsibility carried—may be measured by the maximum span of time during which he is authorised to exercise discretion on his own account. The measure is adduced by the period of time in which he is required to exercise his own discretion without being subject to check or review by someone who holds authority over him. When level of work is measured in this manner—I have termed it the time-span of discretion—there can be observed a relationship between the level of work a man is given and the amount of money he expects to earn for that work. This sense of a fair level of pay for any given level of work is uniform from one person to the next, regardless of the kind of work done. In short, there is a general wage and salary scale based on level of work done, which is unconsciously employed and is felt to be fair and equitable.

Earning growth curves can be accurately placed by first measuring the maximum levels of work carried by a man at various stages in his career, and then substituting the salary equivalent of that level of work. The curve thus obtained will be found to conform to the shape of the normal earning growth curves, and the relevant earning curve for the individual can be discovered. Upward or downward deviations in actual earnings may then be observed.

It may be noted that our earning growth curve represents the increasing level of payment we seek consistent with the progressive growth in our capacity for higher levels of work. This capacity is not just intellectual capacity. It is a combination of our intellectual capacity to judge and to decide, and our emotional capacity to act with decision and to tolerate the burden of uncertainty while awaiting the results of decisions made during the period discretion is being exercised.

The Conflict between Unconscious and Conscious Evaluations of Work

This statement of our unconscious knowledge of the degree of consistency between our capacity, work, and earnings, and of the sense of balance and of peace of mind with respect to them we tend to experience when we judge all three to be in line with each other, may be at variance with everyday notions and with customary ways of talking about these matters. Work and money are so commonly the source of phantasies and daydreams of wealth and creativity, comfort and security, greatness and power—or, in contrast, of masochistic phantasies of failure, impotence, and destructiveness. Our conscious self-evaluation and ambitions may be subject to gross fluctuation from depressed self-contempt to omnipotent aggrandisement, according to our mood as affected by our unconscious phantasies. Thus we may all have experience of individuals whose thinking was dominated by phantasy—

consciously and unconsciously—for greater or shorter periods in their careers, and who made a failure of it.

There is an apparent paradox in our outlook. Our unconscious knowledge of our capacity is realistic and stable. Our conscious self-evaluation—connected with unconscious phantasy as well as with unconscious knowledge—may be irrational and emotionally unstable. Unconscious knowledge and the dictates of phantasy may be at odds. These conflicts between the demands of reality and of phantasy have been elaborated by Freud into one of the keystones of his thoughts on the ultimate problems of life—his theory of the conflict between the pleasure principle and the reality principle in human behaviour (2). This theory can be applied with benefit to the analysis of behaviour at work.

Freud has described how under the influence of the pleasure principle, adjusted to a primary mode of operation, pain is evaded and immediate gratification of impulses is sought. The demands of self-preservation, however, lead to the partial replacement of the pleasure principle by the reality principle. We give up our striving for immediate gratification of whatever impulse happens to feel most urgent. The limitations of what is possible in reality are recognised and accepted, and temporary pain and frustration are endured. Eventual satisfaction is by this means assured—satisfaction within the limits afforded by reality, but real satisfaction and not the substitute gratification of phantasy which in the end cannot satisfy genuine material needs.

At work especially the requirements of reality have to be subserved—continued employment and survival depend upon it. If anyone takes on work at a level above his capacity, he eventually fails in his work. If he accepts a level of work below his capacity, he meets the resistance of his innate need to express his creativity and to avoid impotence. He also meets the external resistance of his colleagues, his superiors, and his subordinates (if any), who will not tolerate the disequilibrium in organisation and in payment structure caused by someone occupying a position at a level below the capacity he can exercise. In short, each one is subject to a strong field of force tending to keep him in a position at a level of work consistent with his capacity.

It is our reality sense responding to this external field of force which produces our unconscious knowledge of the level of work we can successfully carry. For external reality to be accurately perceived and retained even unconsciously requires that there has been a sufficient working-through of what Melanie Klein has termed infantile paranoid and depressive anxieties. (I shall have more to say in a moment about this topic.) With sufficient reduction of these anxieties integration of the ego becomes sufficiently well established for the reality principle to operate, and appreciation of experience at work is possible.

It would appear that anyone who is capable of earning his own living has developed a sufficient degree of inner reality to be able to make the unconscious judgment of his work-capacity about which I am speaking. But this does not mean that the assessment of our real capacity is consciously accepted. Quite the contrary. Very few of us are capable of tolerating consciously an accurate and stable self-appraisal of our capacities and limitations. Some of our deepest unconscious defences against anxiety would be threatened— phantasy gratification, omnipotence, self-effacement. We repress our knowledge of our true capacity, and retain it repressed in our unconscious mind. This repression allows emotional oscillations in our conscious self-evaluation, while at the same time maintaining our unconscious knowledge of our adjustment to work reality. It is only in the exceptional naturally mature and integrated person that much of the unconscious knowledge of capacity becomes conscious. Consciously realistic self-appraisal is also a condition to be hoped for in a successful personal analysis.

With respect to payment for capacity and level of work, similar forces come into play. Payment above or below the level of work carried means that greater or lesser relative payment is being received by others—by colleagues, by superiors, by subordinates, or by those working in other parts of the establishment or in other establishments. These deviations inevitably become public—through positions falling vacant and having to be advertised, through newcomers bringing standards from elsewhere, or simply through comparisons of earning with colleagues and friends. Overpayment stimulates pressure from others to regain a situation of equilibrium. Underpayment stimulates pressure in oneself.

If the above observations are accurate, then much of the upheaval and disturbance about differentials (including economically devastating strikes) would appear to be resolvable if we could tap the unconscious knowledge of individuals. If we were each allocated increasing responsibility according to the unconsciously perceived growth in our own capacity, much heart-burning and disaffection might be avoided. And if we were each paid on the basis of the correct wage or salary for the level of work we carried, then much of the acute social disequilibrium and greed provoked by invidious rivalries over differentials could be obviated. Such a move might mean planned and foreseen changes in occupation if a person outran the level of work available in his existing job; but our full-employment economy has provided plenty of opportunity for our making changes of this kind.

The solution, however, is far from being so easy—as is readily appreciated from our actual experience of industrial strife. Our behaviour is not solely determined by such rational considerations. Unconscious phantasies and impulses seek gratification as well. And unconscious conflicts and anxieties produce pain and suffering. Because these processes are unconscious, they cannot be brought under the dominion of the reality-principle in mental functioning. The unconscious needs for gratification and for avoidance of frustration and pain, expressed under the code of the pleasure-principle, do not tolerate delay. They provoke immediate and compulsive forms of behaviour which, because they are unconsciously admixed with our more rational and controlled objectives, may often be self-defeating in their effect.

Working and striving for a particular standard of living, revive and reactivate some of the most primitive and deep-

lying of these unconscious phantasies. These primitive phantasies, at work in the adult mind, are now much more
clearly understood as a result of work stemming from Freud
—notably the work in this country of Melanie Klein (3). I
shall combine some of the broad outlines of their conclusions
with examples from industry which I have had the opportunity frequently to observe in order to illustrate the revival
of these primitive phantasies in our work relationships.

Unconscious Anxieties affecting our Behaviour at Work

In the unconscious mind, work, ambition, and desire for
material gain and security revive unconscious phantasies of
infantile activities and the primitive relationships with
parental figures. When employment is satisfactory—when it
is interesting and fairly remunerated, and when opportunity
exists for progress at a rate compatible with personal development—it will tend to revive the satisfactions and unconscious
constructive and creative impulses established in infancy
under the influence of good feeding and experiences, and good
loving impulses. The extent to which good morale may be
created when work is satisfactory will depend on the strength
of the primitive feelings of love and co-operativeness in the
unconscious mind. In the absence or near absence of any
such positive unconscious feelings, psychotic or severe psycho-
pathic personality development occurs of a kind which re-
duces the capacity to work to zero or near zero—and con-
sideration of such conditions is outside our present scope.

But even when work is experienced as good, it may not
revive good unconscious memories alone. It may also revive
unconscious feelings of guilt and of depressive anxiety—the
residues of infantile phantasies of the destruction and loss of
the good aspects of primitive objects as a result of aggressive
and sadistic attacks upon these objects. Added to these
depressive anxieties are the deep and strong paranoid
anxieties which may be revived in the unconscious mind by
the unsatisfactory features—and these are always present—in
our work. These paranoid anxieties are established in the
deep layers of the unconscious as a result of the projection

into external objects of the young infant's greedy and destructive impulses—the external objects seeming the more
dangerous and persecuting the stronger the infant's impulses
and the more frustrating its external circumstances.

These very deep-lying paranoid and depressive anxieties
are present to some extent in each of us, constituting a
vaguely felt threat to our sanity, and indeed to our existence.
They show themselves in our work, for example, in the unconscious response of managers and subordinates to the fact
that they are mutually dependent. This dependence readily
invokes unconscious feelings of hostility and persecution,
such that victimisation and unfair practices are commonly
anticipated to an extent which may be out of all proportion
to the real situation. The giving and receiving of instructions,
consciously accepted and desired as necessary for getting
work out, nevertheless creates conflict at the unconscious
level. Receiving an instruction is experienced as being subjected to persecuting omnipotence on the part of one's man-
ager. Giving an instruction is experienced as wielding destructive and sadistic power. Paranoid anxiety in the receiver
of orders, and depressive anxiety in the giver of them, are
important reasons why the exercise of authority is chronically
experienced as difficult.

In like vein, deep-lying passions of envy may be expressed.
In the infantile unconscious, as Mrs Klein has recently
shown (4), envy is directed against the parent's possession of
creativity and adult peace of mind; it arouses intense impulses to spoil that creativity and peace of mind. In adult
work, envy may manifest itself as envy of the person in the
superior position who is perceived as creative and free. It
may also be manifest as envy of those in subordinate positions
who are perceived as having peace of mind because of lesser
responsibility. In either case, unconscious envy is provocative
of wrangling and perturbation in the relationship between
superiors and subordinates.

Unconscious rivalry also plays its part as well as conscious
rivalry. In omnipotent phantasy, parents are surpassed, their
positions and their possessions are usurped; sibling rivals—

the unborn ones as well as the living—are defeated and destroyed; and a state of complete gratification is achieved. At work these phantasies express themselves in omnipotent feelings (operating at all levels in executive systems) that one could do the other's job so much better, or warrants the higher job if only ability were what counted. More concretely, they are observable in the notorious difficulties which surround promotion and advancement procedures.

Unconscious Collusion in Group Relationships

Such, then, are examples of the unconscious impulses and conflicts which co-exist with the more reality-determined components of our behaviour. How, then, do we get control of the anxieties which accompany these unconscious processes? To some extent we counteract the anxieties by repression, and by a variety of psychological mechanisms within the individual, as, for example, sublimation. But they are rarely to be completely coped with in such a manner. Attempts to reduce the pain and anxiety of these unconscious phantasies may result in neurotic behaviour under the influence of the pleasure principle. In our work, such influences may provoke not only phantasies of greater success or failure, but may provoke the actual seeking of employment, or of payment, out of keeping with the unconsciously known limits of our capacity.

But of greater importance for our immediate purpose is the fact that these anxieties and impulses may be externalised and played out in group life. It was Freud, in his great studies of group psychology (5), who showed how we unconsciously identify with each other, live parts of our lives by identification with the behaviour of others and by taking these others and their behaviour as parts of ourselves. We enter into what I would term unconscious collusion with each other so as to pool unwanted and painful parts of our unconscious lives in group relationships. The operation of unconscious influences in economic life has long been familiar to economic and political scientists—Keynes, for example, making frequent reference to the unconscious instinctive reactions influencing the expectation of income, the propensity to consume, and the inducement to invest.

At workshop level, the unconscious collusive relationships can be observed, for example, in exaggerated 'flaps' and crises about production, or in objectively uncalled for stresses between groups and between individuals, such as those I described earlier.

Or there may be unconscious denial and concealment of actual difficulties. The collusive element shows in the manner in which aspects of reality are denied all round, the resulting confused situation, for example, enabling managers and workers alike—directly and through their representatives—to see each other as persecuting and persecuted, guilty and injured.

But it is the larger-scale aspects of economic organisation which provide the farthest removed and the most impersonal screen for the projection of paranoid and depressive phantasies and anxieties. Socially sanctioned and well-established stereotypes of groups and of individuals, however inaccurate these stereotypes may be, serve admirably to represent figures of the unconscious mind—whether idealised or persecuting. There is full scope, for instance, justifiably to take sides for or against, when group conflict exists, and by this means to live out one's internal conflicts through identification with a conflict which can be observed to exist outside.

This kind of projection of internal conflict by individuals in the mass has the most disturbing effect on the stability and sanity of our economic and industrial arrangements. It plays havoc with any basis of reality-assessment in these arrangements. It is quite incredible, for example, to what extent the reality of level of work is ignored in wage negotiations, despite the fact that agreements are supposedly made on the basis of what is referred to as the 'rate for the job'. The great railway strike of last summer is a good example of what commonly happens. The payment differential between the footplatemen and the porters had lessened—the payment gap had closed. And so it was argued that the footplatemen had been losing. But there was no evidence considered as to what had happened to the relative levels of work of these two classes of worker. Had their work changed over the years? For, if the differential in level of work between the foot-platemen and the porters had dropped in the same proportion as the differential in payment, then there was no real change in the situation. In the absence of evidence about level of work, the argument about payment could not be resolved in principle. It was resolved finally by intuitive judgment about level of work, whatever the supposed basis of the discussions.

The extent to which phantasy can override reality was also shown in the widely used and accepted argument that locomotive drivers were responsible for the safety of hundreds of passengers and for countless thousands of pounds' worth of property. The reward for this supposed responsibility was to be an increase to a minimum wage of some £10 per week. The disjunction in thought needs only to be pointed out to be self-evident. A moment's reflection makes it clear that in fact no discretion which could affect lives is left to the driver. The safety system works according to a set of prescribed rules, non-conformance to these rules constituting negligence. Objective examination of any work situation will demonstrate that we simply do not make payment relative to the possible consequences of negligence. Yet in the heat of conflict we readily and publicly discuss and argue the ludicrous as though it were fact.

Comparisons for negotiation purposes are usually made in terms of people and not of work—the value of miners as against machinists, of typographers as against unskilled workers, and (recently) the value of those in the so-called middle-class occupations as against the value of the skilled artisan working-classes. These methods of negotiation are well-suited to the unconscious need for having invidious and, inevitably, destructive comparisons publicly made between individuals, between occupational groups, and between classes of society.

In the absence of any objective yardstick for comparing

responsibilities, executive leadership is inverted. Waiting for dissatisfaction to arise becomes a basic technique for adjusting and regulating payment. When employees become sufficiently dissatisfied with their pay, they are expected to ask for more. Initiative is expected from below rather than from above. And the various groups are left to fight out their own differentials, with the employers sitting by, apparently helpless, but unconsciously taking part in the shambles through having relinquished their initiative. The consequence is a discrediting of authority, and an enfeeblement of leadership—a familiar problem in contemporary society.

It will be noted in all our examples that the maintenance of the unconsciously motivated difficulties depends upon the constant repression of the unconsciously grasped relationship between level of work, of capacity, and a national scale of earnings. Without this unconsciously collusive repression and denial, the more chaotic, compulsive, and confused aspects of our economic relationships would be lost. But their loss would also mean the loss by the individual of a great defence against psychotic anxiety—for it is precisely these seemingly irrational and chaotic features which contain and reflect the mass projections from our unconscious minds. I say seemingly irrational, for their logic is the logic of the unconscious.

The Control of Unconscious Social Collusions

How, then, are these social processes akin to mass psychotic phenomena to be kept under control? They are limited by two factors: the co-existence of processes operating under the reality principle; and the fact that the chaos induced to relieve unconscious pain itself becomes too painful to endure. The demands of reality and of economic survival, of the individual and of the group, eventually force compromise and resolution, and a return to temporary states of equilibrium. The individual cannot make a living if he indulges in wholesale neurotic behaviour in his work. In the workshop and the office, for any enterprise to survive, a minimum good working relationship is necessary in the day-to-day work situation between managers and workers, and between colleagues. At national level, the impact of economic and work reality, intuitively perceived and understood, forces eventual solutions despite the emotional and irrational impulses at work in all parties to the dispute.

But it is fast becoming apparent that the reality principle operating at the unconscious level cannot necessarily be counted upon to take effect quickly enough to avoid serious disturbance to our industrial economy while disputes are in progress. The final results of wage negotiations are too often achieved in spite of, rather than because of, the manifest content of the arguments brought to bear and the methods of negotiation used. A distorted and unrealistic perception of economic motivation, work, and payment has become established in the public mind. And the fabric of leadership is torn, managers and workers alike finding themselves at a loss to discover those principles on which challenging and acceptable leadership and initiative can be exerted with respect to work and payment.

But our analysis suggests that there are unexpectedly profound difficulties in the way of change. Unless we individually become better able to deal with our unconscious anxieties, any decrease in the use of unconscious collusions in industry will only cause a displacement of projection and of chaos into other group situations. Yet widespread change in individuals is clearly too much to be hoped for. Such change means each one achieving a deeper relationship with himself, an increased awareness and understanding of his internal reality. And it is precisely this contact with our inner world which has always proved difficult; the threat of madness from the unconscious psychotic anxieties we bear causes us to recoil from too much personal insight and sense of reality. Nevertheless, a growth in insight and understanding in those who presume to positions of leadership and high responsibility would be of great practical value. They at least might come to grips within themselves with the forces which distort their sense of reality and, without their being aware of it, cause them to take part in the collusive arrangements to deny reality at the social level, and, indeed, unwittingly to lead such collusion.

A change to reality-based leadership means the application of methods for arranging payments in a manner precisely consistent with the level of work we are each given to carry, and work consistent with our capacity. (Our evidence suggests that the development and use of these methods is not too difficult—if we can get away from our unconscious anxiety-distorted social conception of the economic world.) Such leadership would make contact with our unconscious knowledge and inner reality. It would encourage a sense of satisfaction and peace of mind. This is not to say that any such arrangement would automatically eliminate unhappiness and neurosis. But it would mean that our work would not be one more force in itself stimulating emotional disturbance. It would at least act in the direction of stimulating in each of us as much satisfaction and peace of mind as our personality make-up and other life circumstances can allow.

Furthermore, such arrangements might enable us to find our way out of the spur to inflation caused by not having any objective standard of level of work against which to pitch, and hold firm, a satisfactory pattern of payment differentials. The alleviation of problems of differentials could effect a lessening of the destructive rivalries between groups and between classes. Publicly sanctioned acceptance of reality as a basis for considering work could allow for more satisfactory and constructive leadership. It could add to our national store of sanity. It could strengthen our national morale.

In concluding, I recognise that this analysis may be felt to lead to an essentially pessimistic outcome. But this view is not necessarily warranted. By the discovery of his techniques, Freud has made it a practical matter to gain genuine and conscious insight into the deeper recesses of our own minds. Through the theories which he and his successors have elaborated by the use of these techniques, a conscious intellectual and scientific understanding of social problems may become possible. To fail to direct our social endeavours towards greater reality based on insight is to encourage the burgeoning of the psychotic state, a state which readily calls forth its psychotic leaders. As against such a cataclysm, increasing social sanity can gradually be gained—but only if we recognise mass unconscious social collusions for what they are and bring them under the control of conscious and mature insight.

BIBLIOGRAPHY

(1) JAQUES, E.(1956). *Measurement of Responsibility*. London: Tavistock Publications.

(2) FREUD, S., *Beyond the Pleasure Principle*. London: Hogarth Press, 1922.

(3) See, for example, KLEIN, MELANIE (Ed.) (1955). *New Directions in Psycho-Analysis*. London: Tavistock Publications.

(4) KLEIN, MELANIE (1957). *Envy and Gratitude*. London: Tavistock Publications.

(5) FREUD, S., *Group Psychology and the Analysis of the Ego*. London: Hogarth Press, 1940.

VII

A CHARACTER TRAIT OF FREUD'S

By JOAN RIVIERE

ALWAYS one of the most interesting things to me about Freud was his writing; I met him first in his writings before I knew him. You get an impression of the man from them, quite apart from the impression their content makes on you. As is well known, his style and presentation are very different from that of most scientific writers. (Actually, Freud's writings do vary and are of more than one description, but I am speaking now of the style which predominates and characterises the main volume of his work.) Its general character is not only direct and plain-spoken—simple statements without padding—but in particular it conveys vividly an awareness of his readers or hearers, as if he were speaking directly to them, and were concerned to put forward his views in a form intelligible to *them*. The structure of his argument is not built up in a vacuum, as it were; it has a direct reference to the reader; he is addressing you. There is a personal quality, a personal relation, implicit in his style.

When I came to know Freud himself, however, I found that he did not appear especially interested in impressing himself on people or in seeking to convince others of his views. We know that he needed the support of an outside recognition and the acceptance of his work; he hoped for it, but in everyday life he appeared to take no direct steps to obtain it. There seemed to be a paradox here: on the one hand he had no strong impulse to influence others, to teach or convince them—not even in fact a marked interest in curing them, as he has told us; the aim of impressing himself on people seemed to be lacking or minimal in him. Yet he had developed this special capacity for presenting his conclusions as if he were bent on enabling the reader to take them in—so much so that it colours his whole style and gives the presentation a simplicity and lucidity (often when the content is obscure) that is peculiar to him and most rare in such work.

I wondered about this paradox and why he had this relation to his readers—as if they and *their* thoughts were an essential factor in the process of formulating his views.

He once said something to me which had little meaning for me at the time but which later threw light on this problem for me. I suppose I had mentioned some analytic explanation that had occurred to me. He said: 'Write it, write it, put it down in black and white; that's the way to deal with it; you get it out of your system.' I didn't feel that this prescription meant much to me, and it fell by the way. It must obviously have been true for him, however, and I remembered it. In later years, as I acquired more knowledge and understanding of him and his work, and especially under the stimulus of his biography, I came more and more to realise the underlying importance in him of the creative side of his work—his work must have meant to him a structure he was building and creating. He almost says so once or twice. This idea then linked up in my mind with his former remark to me: 'Get it out, produce it, make something of it—*outside you*, that is; give it an existence independently of you.'

He clearly did not consciously or explicitly think of his work as creative; as we all do, he thought of it as scientific, as discovery or acquisition of facts and knowledge, which indeed it is. But when we look at the vast fabric he raised, it is evident that even his unique capacity to recognise facts would in itself not have produced the great body of knowledge he left us. It was a deeper impulse in him—a capacity to construct and create something, a living body, to build up outside himself a body of knowledge that comprehends the single facts of which it is formed and yet transcends them, thus becoming an independent whole in itself—it was this that played such a notable part in his work. There was a marriage in him of the seeker after existing

truth and the creator giving the world a new living truth—
the scientist and the artist in one. The outcome represents
a fusion of external reality and internal phantasy, in which
each contributes to fulfilling the aims of the other as well as
its own. And the extremely high degree of satisfaction that
results when this fulfilment is achieved betokens, I believe,
the essence of that quality we call greatness.

As I see it, then, the act of writing his ideas, of conveying
them, putting them over into the minds of others, represented
a process of building up those ideas into a whole outside himself and inside the minds of others. His concern was not
primarily to obtain their acceptance; primarily he was engaged on an act of creation in which his hearers and readers
were his medium, his vehicle in the process, as well as both
the source and the abode of his creation. When the new
living body was born, it had been shaped and framed and
housed in other minds outside his. This for me explains the
paradox that in ordinary life Freud had no great interest in
directly influencing another person, but that what he was
interested to do, consciously or not, was to work out and
construct the edifice of his thought into an intelligible
whole by means of their co-operation and their thought.
And for this he had to make his direct personal appeal to
them in plain and simple terms.

I said in simple terms. Freud's simplicity was a familiar
characteristic to those who knew him, yet it is something
very hard to convey. One tends to think of this great man
who produced this immense volume of work in his lifetime,
and who was occupied with such totally new, unheard-of,
and sometimes obscure ideas, as a completely sophisticated
being, surveying the world and the objects of his study from
a detached distance. It is quite untrue; behind the dignity
and reserve of a serious, much-occupied professional man,
he was a most unsophisticated person and sometimes quite
naïve. Ernest Jones has quoted evidences of it in the biography. He was not a man of the world, though he was in no
way retiring or withdrawn, and he was not a judge of men.
He habitually reacted with simple spontaneous naturalness

to whatever he met, on the assumption that whatever he perceived was valid in itself. Nothing else concerned him at the moment. He established an instantaneous, direct relation to his perception, which automatically excluded cut-and-dried assumptions, or *arrière-pensées*. Second thoughts and suspended judgment only came much later. The impulse to reject and dismiss at first sight was singularly lacking in him. In using the word naïveté of him, in spite of its usual rather disparaging connotation, I have done so because it alone, I feel, conveys the strength of this immediate acceptance of whatever he met with as valid. It was this quality which enabled him to by-pass the scepticism of an ordinary physician about the patients' Oedipus phantasies and to perceive the element of reality in them; just as it was this capacity that had led to the brilliant results of his study of dreams. One could say that his simple direct personal response to whatever he perceived as valid in itself was the unique characteristic of his genius; other faculties of his others have also had, perhaps no one else had this as he had it.

And so by these means and in this way he gradually discovered the unconscious. First he thought of it as a storehouse of memories; then he discovered its character as the mental side of the instincts we are born with, those dynamic forces in us which issue in all our emotions, actions and behaviour, thoughts and feelings, and activate them. He saw the unconscious as the connecting-link—the clearinghouse, as it were—between these biological forces of instinct and the conscious life of adult men and women. He bent his energies to building up for us in his writings a picture of this world which is unknown to us and yet is so powerful in determining our lives. Only if we can recognise it can we make better use of it; for we do not know of it, and we protect ourselves from doing so largely by thinking of it as in other people's minds! I think in analysis it is as necessary to keep in mind how strong the *not* seeing and *not* knowing is in us as to learn all we can about what is unconscious in the mind.

What I am speaking of now springs from another of Freud's sayings to me. In my analysis he one day made some interpretation, and I responded to it by an objection. He then said: 'It is *un-conscious*.' I was overwhelmed then by the realisation that I knew nothing about it—I knew nothing about it. In that instant he had created in me his discovery of the powerful unconscious in our minds that we know nothing of, and that yet is impelling and directing us. I have never forgotten this reminder from him of what unconscious means.

In the Museum of Maya Culture